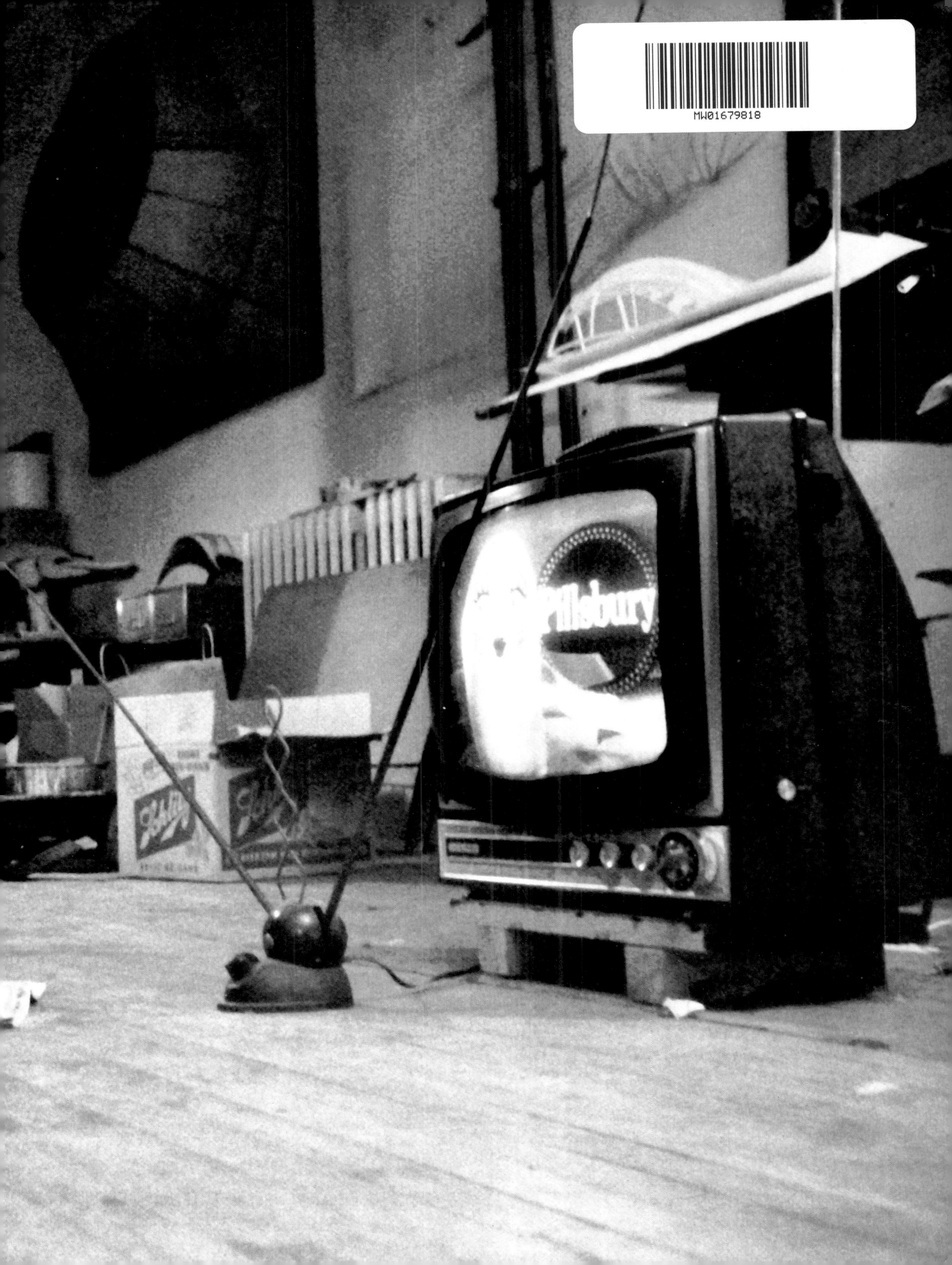
Pillsbury

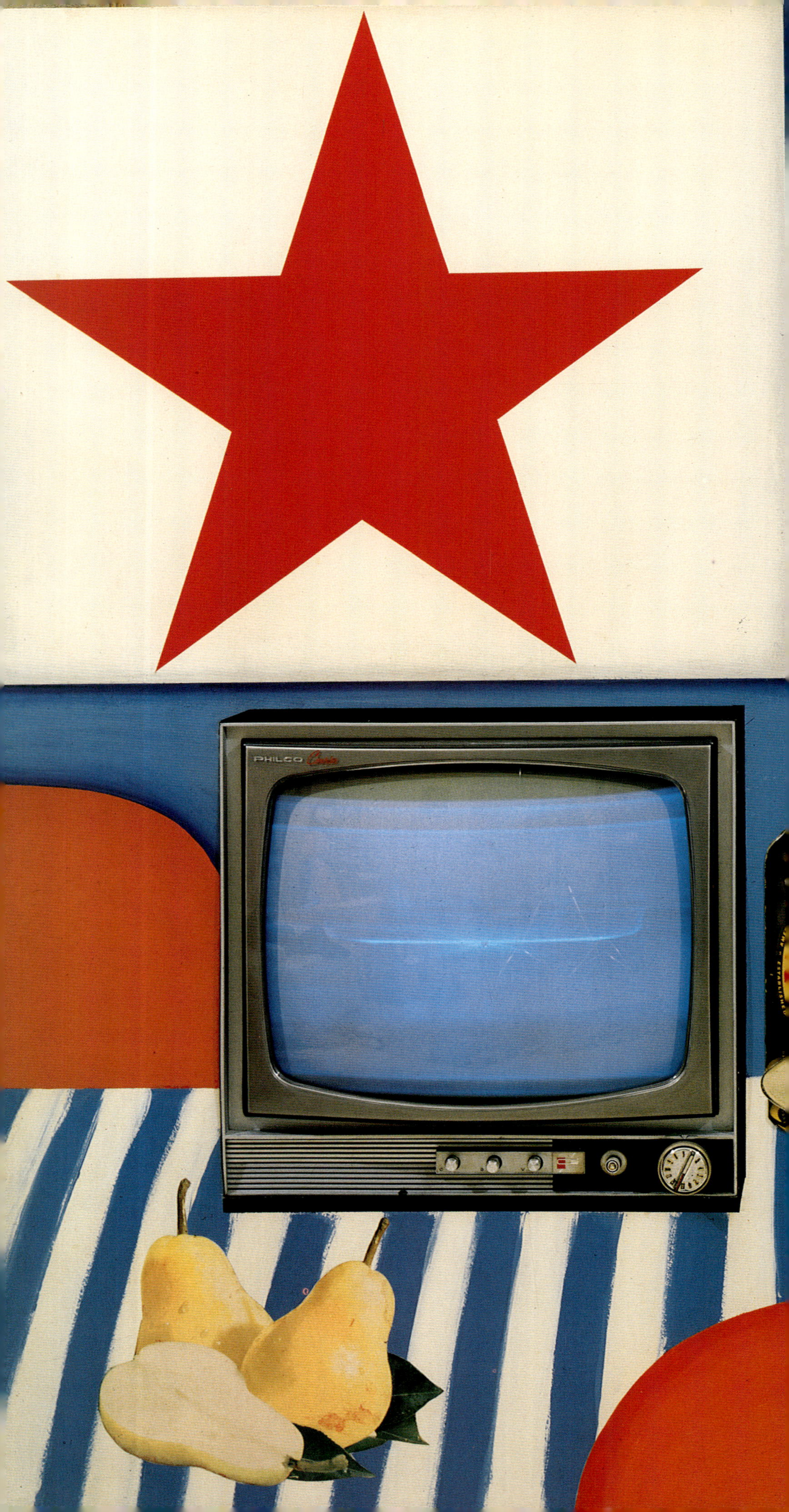
PHILCO

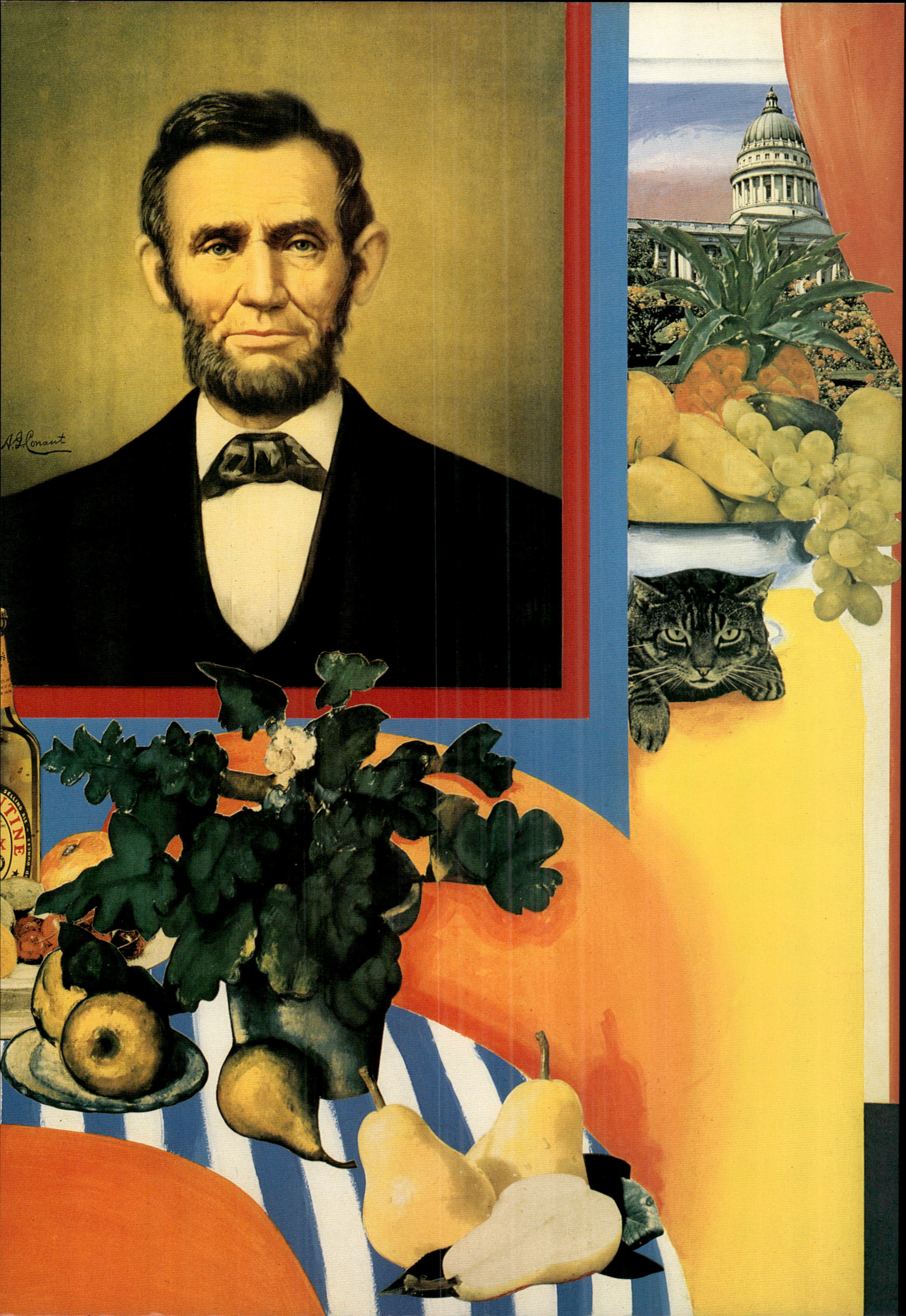
A.J. Conant

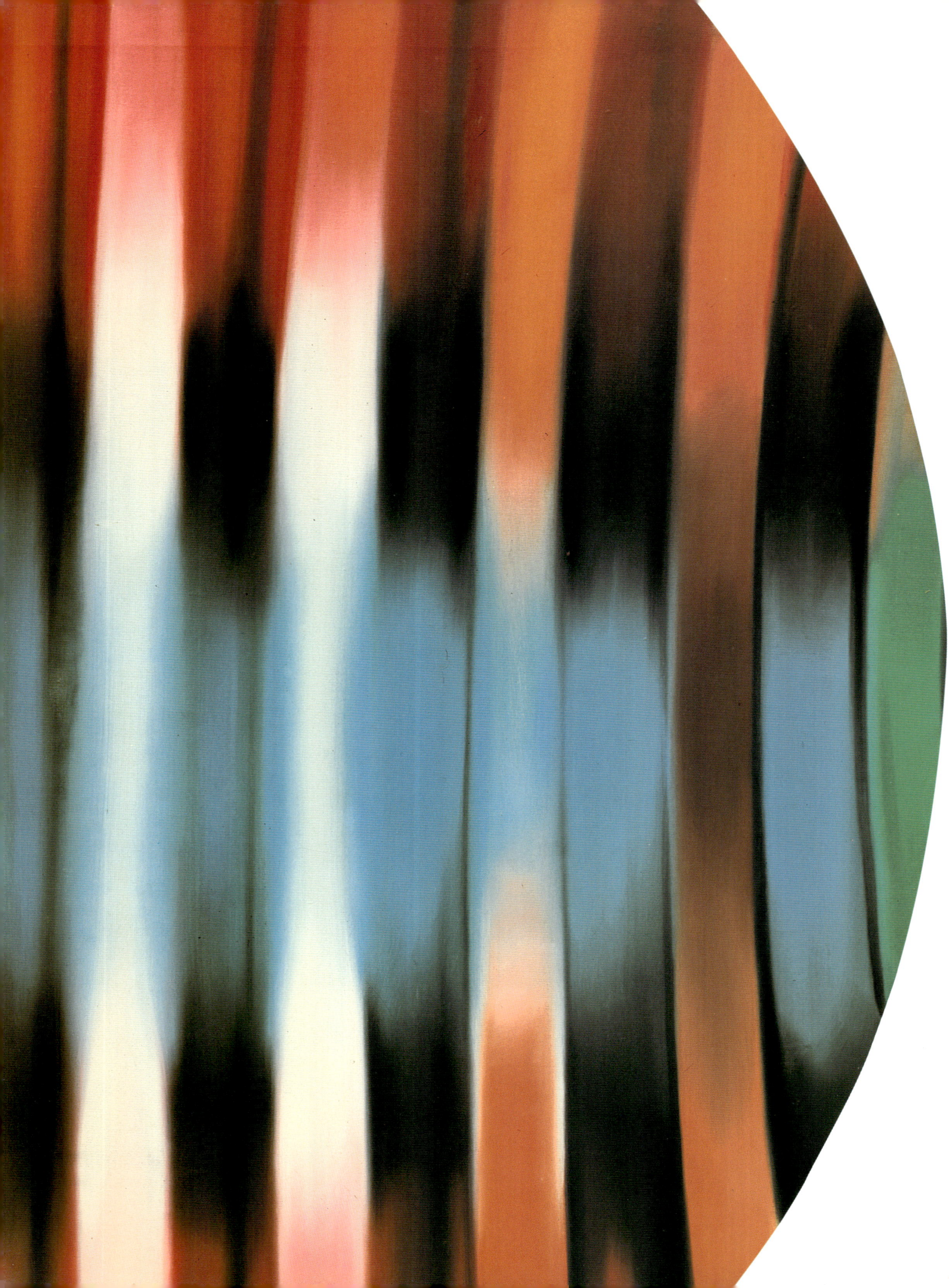

The New Frontier

ART AND TELEVISION 1960·65

Curated by John Alan Farmer

Austin Museum of Art
Austin, Texas, 2000

This catalogue has been published on the occasion of the exhibition *The New Frontier: Art and Television, 1960–65*, guest curated by John Alan Farmer, and organized by the Austin Museum of Art.

Austin Museum of Art
823 Congress Avenue, Austin, Texas
September 1–November 26, 2000

Major support for this exhibition and catalogue was provided by

AT&T

Additional support was provided by Arthur Frakes.

The Austin Museum of Art is funded in part by the City of Austin, under the auspices of the Austin Arts Commission, and the Texas Commission on the Arts. Additional support is generously provided by Members of the Museum and the Austin Museum of Art Guild.

American Airlines is the official airline and The Driskill is the official hotel of the Austin Museum of Art. Promotional sponsors include *The Austin Chronicle*, 107.1 KGSR, and Pentagram Design.

ISBN Number 0-9670952-2-0
Library of Congress Card Number 00-103945

Published by the Austin Museum of Art, P.O. Box 1847, Austin, Texas 78767. www.amoa.org

Design and typography: Russell Hassell, New York
Publication Coordinator and Editor: Lisa Dirks
Printer: The Studley Press Inc., Dalton, Massachusetts

Front Cover:
Lee Friedlander, *Washington, D.C.*, 1962 (detail), Courtesy Fraenkel Gallery, San Francisco

Inside Front Cover:
Ugo Mulas, Untitled (Lee Bontecou watching television in her studio in New York City), ca. 1965 (detail) Archivio Ugo Mulas, Milan

Page 2–3:
Tom Wesselmann, *Still Life #28*, 1963, Collection of Robert E. Abrams

Frontispiece:
James Rosenquist, *Aspen, Colorado*, 1966 (detail), Private Collection, Courtesy Sonnabend Gallery, New York

Page 8:
Andy Warhol, *Jackie*, 1964, (One painting from the series), The Andy Warhol Museum, Pittsburgh, Founding Collection, Contribution The Andy Warhol Foundation for the Visual Arts, Inc.

Page 15:
K. O. Götz, *Statistisch-metrische Modulation 12:2:1*, 1960 (detail), Collection of the artist

Page 102–103:
Peter Moore, Nam June Paik with original *Demagnetizer* (or *Life Ring*), New York, October 1965 (detail), Courtesy Estate of Peter Moore/Bound & Unbound, New York

Inside Back Cover:
Andy Warhol, *Outer and Inner Space*, 1965 (film stills, detail), The Andy Warhol Museum, Pittsburgh

Back Cover:
Nam June Paik, *Zen for TV*, 1963/2000 Collection of the Austin Museum of Art

Lenders

Robert E. Abrams

Galerie Berndt Kunsthandel GmbH, Cologne

Bruce Conner and Canyon Cinema

Fraenkel Gallery, San Francisco

K. O. Götz, Niederbreitbach-Wolfenacker, Germany

Art Collection, Harry Ransom Humanities Research Center, The University of Texas at Austin

Jon and Joanne Hendricks, New York

Dennis Hopper

Nicole Klagsbrun Gallery, New York

The Mayor Gallery, London

The Menil Collection, Houston

Estate of Peter Moore/Bound & Unbound, New York

Archivio Ugo Mulas, Milan

The Museum of Modern Art Library, New York

Museum of Modern Art Ludwig Foundation Vienna

Rare Books and Manuscripts, The Ohio State University Libraries, Columbus

Collection Onnasch, Berlin

Yoko Ono, New York

Tony Shafrazi Gallery, New York

The Gilbert and Lila Silverman Fluxus Collection, Detroit

The Sixth Floor Museum at Dealey Plaza, Dallas

Fine Art Rafael Vostell, Berlin

The Andy Warhol Museum, Pittsburgh

Weatherspoon Art Gallery, The University of North Carolina at Greensboro

William S. Wilson, New York

An Anonymous Lender

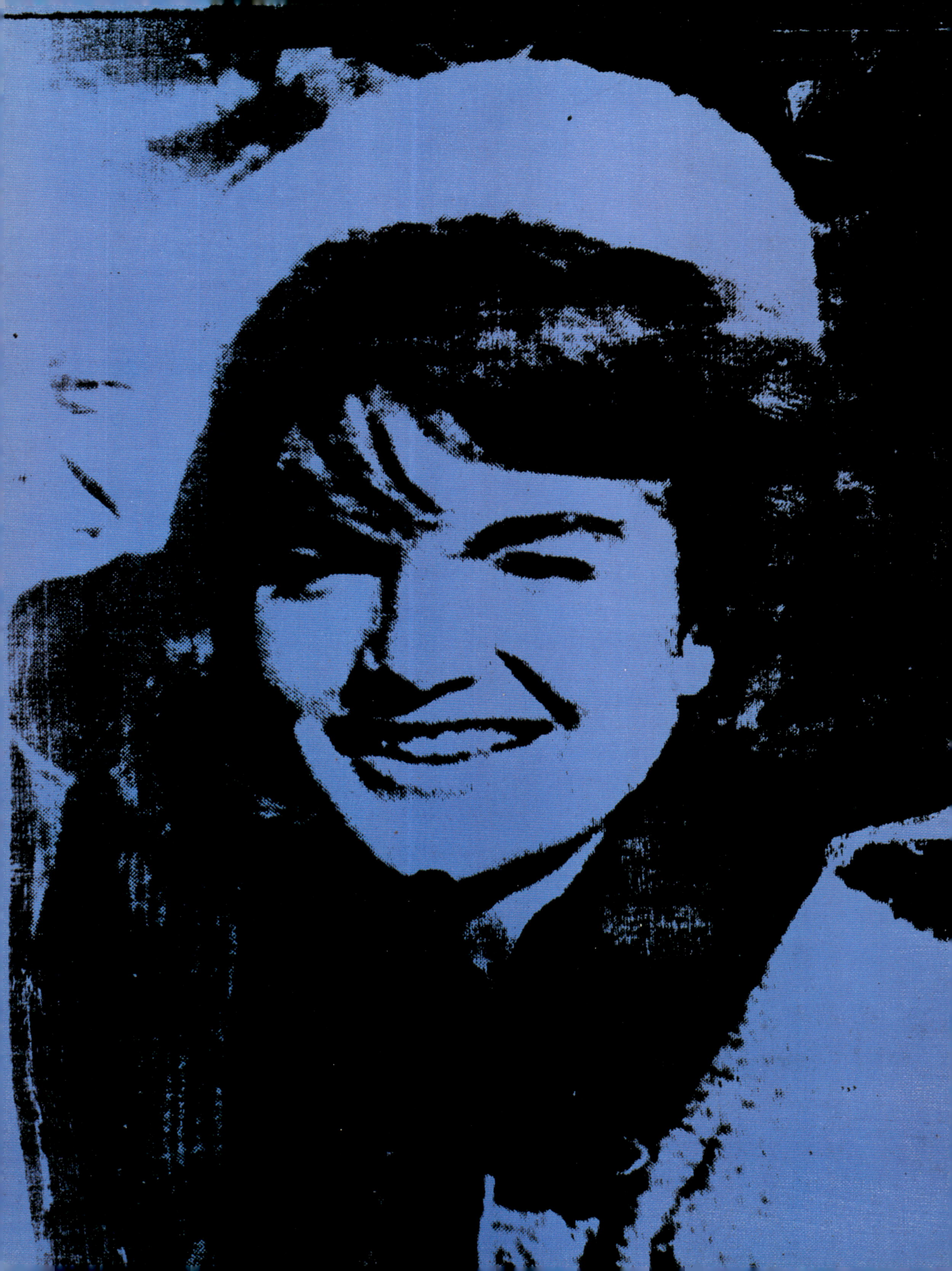

Contents

Foreword

The term "The New Frontier" was coined by advisers to John F. Kennedy during the 1960 presidential campaign. It was intended to conjure, among other things, not only the vast territories of outer space awaiting discovery through American initiative, but also those regions of the Cold War world that were perceived to welcome United States democracy and prosperity. There was, however, another territory opening up at this time, one that would eventually prove to be far more vast and complex, and that would come to mark indelibly late-twentieth-century culture throughout the world. In the early 1960s, for the first time, a majority of Americans viewed images that emanated from within the television set, embedding themselves in a uniquely profound way in individual consciousness through their ubiquity, repetition, and transmission into the intimacy of the home. As John Alan Farmer, guest curator of *The New Frontier: Art and Television, 1960–65*, points out in the essay that follows, the ability of television in the early 1960s to transmit live images endowed the medium with a visual and cultural authority that the world had not known until that time. This perspective may be difficult for us to appreciate today, in an age characterized by cynicism and immersion in that very medium.

The desire of the artists included in the exhibition to explore a phenomenon as pervasive, encompassing, and at that time as recent as television, must be considered ambitious and farsighted. Theirs was an ambition fueled by a fresh curiosity about the quotidian icons and materials of popular culture and by a desire to incorporate new media into the practice of making art. The pioneering artists featured in *The New Frontier: Art and Television, 1960–65*—Robert Rauschenberg, Andy Warhol, Bruce Conner, and Nam June Paik, among others—were part of a new generation that disavowed the aesthetic values of Abstract Expressionism. With its emphasis on the primacy of the individual quest for personal and spiritual expression and the grand emotional gesture, Abstract Expressionism dominated the artistic landscape in the United States and Western Europe during the 1950s. Heroic, large-scale painting was its preferred and most exalted form, reconstituting the earlier romantic definition of the artist as someone outside the boundaries of society's norms. By contrast, artists in the early 1960s focused energetically, even pragmatically, on social issues that were then beginning to surface in the United States. If it can be said that art first registers the tremors of societal change, then the work about television produced by Wolf Vostell, Ed Kienholz, Garry Winogrand, and Wallace Berman foreshadowed in the prosperous early part of the decade latent ambiguities and divisions that would manifest in full force during the Vietnam War. It was in this era that television's live quality, its insistent repetition of images, and its daily transmission of events on the evening news mobilized a generation of youth into social action.

An important component of *The New Frontier* is its examination of the role that screens have come to assume in our daily lives. The television screens of the large sets that commanded a central place in living rooms of the period were seen as an authoritative source of news and cultural values, much as radio and, before that, the storyteller had been. Today, the multiplicity and omnipresence of screens—in the form of hand-held wireless devices, LED screens relaying the latest stock market news, cellular telephones, and portable video games—have diffused the family locus and insulated the individual to an even greater extent in his reception and transmission of information, while, ironically, that information is absorbed from ever more widespread and diverse sources.

A subtle shift that occurred in the late 1950s and early 1960s, and one that is most evident in Rauschenberg's silkscreen paintings, was the decline of a model of contemplative viewing with which viewers had traditionally approached a work of art. Rauschenberg appropriated the large-scale canvases of Abstract Expressionism but swept away their symbols, replacing them with kinetic, interacting images that more directly expressed the temper of the new decade. Television's rapid, often abrupt transitions of narratives and context undoubtedly contributed to this change, and in so doing, altered viewers' expectations of what a work of art should communicate.

Another fundamental legacy of television has been its liveness, the effects of which we see today in the huge media events that have characterized the 1990s and the present, from the O. J. Simpson car chase to the accidental deaths and subsequent mourning of Princess Diana and John F. Kennedy, Jr., to the recent custody battle for Elián Gonzalez. The assassination of John F. Kennedy was the first national event in which television played a central role in giving viewers a sense of immediate, personal participation. Through television's focus on the intimate details of the tragedy and its ability to broadcast incidents as the story unfolded, the medium evoked an unprecedented emotional response in the American public. Since then we have seen how a gripping narrative played out in real time has resulted in the conflation of direct experience with the televised image of an event, whose outcome the viewer is incapable of influencing or resolving. For the spectator, this creates a curious kind of experiential limbo characterized by an obsessive repetition of images which often become iconic in the popular imagination but diminish in meaning. Andy Warhol and Bruce Conner both explored this phenomenon in films and prints about Kennedy's assassination and cast a skeptical eye on the underlying themes of voyeurism and manipulation it raised. As John Alan Farmer iterates, power has come to reside more and more insistently in the image of an event rather than in the experience of it. The artists presented in *The New Frontier:*

Art and Television, 1960–65 make us question the evolution of our relationship to television and our future interactions with visual technologies.

My warm thanks and deep appreciation go to John Alan Farmer, the guest curator of *The New Frontier*, for first suggesting the idea for this exhibition more than three years ago. Since then, John has worked energetically and adeptly at transforming the exhibition's themes, which he explored in-depth in his doctoral dissertation, into a show that is both historically important and timely. His perceptive, insightful essay for this catalogue illuminates seminal 1960s artists and their oeuvres in refreshing and unexpected ways.

I would like to extend my sincere gratitude to the lenders to the exhibition, without whose generous support we could not have realized this project: Robert E. Abrams; Galerie Berndt Kunsthandel GmbH, Cologne; Bruce Conner and Canyon Cinema; Fraenkel Gallery, San Francisco; K. O. Götz, Niederbreitbach-Wolfenacker, Germany; Art Collection, Harry Ransom Humanities Research Center, The University of Texas at Austin; Jon and Joanne Hendricks, New York; Dennis Hopper; Nicole Klagsbrun Gallery, New York; The Mayor Gallery, London; The Menil Collection, Houston; Estate of Peter Moore/Bound & Unbound, New York; Archivio Ugo Mulas, Milan; The Museum of Modern Art Library, New York; Museum of Modern Art Ludwig Foundation Vienna, formerly Hahn Collection, Cologne; Rare Books and Manuscripts, The Ohio State University Libraries, Columbus; Collection Onnasch, Berlin; Yoko Ono, New York; Tony Shafrazi Gallery, New York; The Gilbert and Lila Silverman Fluxus Collection, Detroit; The Sixth Floor Museum at Dealey Plaza, Dallas; Fine Art Rafael Vostell, Berlin; The Andy Warhol Museum, Pittsburgh; Weatherspoon Art Gallery, The University of North Carolina at Greensboro; William S. Wilson, New York; and a lender who wishes to remain anonymous.

Numerous individuals worked behind the scenes to make this exhibition possible and were instrumental in its success. I wish to thank the individuals listed below and other staff members at their institutions or organizations: Dorothy Gutterman, Abbeville Press, New York; Lisa Darling and Julia Paull, Alta Light Productions, Venice, California; Caroline Fuchs, Galerie Berndt; David R. Bond, Bond's Television and Electronics, Austin; Neil Waldman, CBS News Archive, New York; Forde Motion Picture Labs, Seattle; Jeffery Fraenkel and Dawn Troy, Fraenkel Gallery; James Silverberg, Goldfarb & Silverberg, Washington, D.C.; Peter Mears and Debra Armstrong-Morgan, Art Collection, Harry Ransom Humanities Research Center, The University of Texas at Austin; Ruth Phaneuf, Nicole Klagsbrun Gallery; Paul Kopeikin, Paul Kopeikin Gallery, Los Angeles; Manfred Leve, Nuremberg, Germany; Stephanie Sherman, LA Louver,

Venice, California; James Mayor and Andrew Murray, The Mayor Gallery; Susan Davidson and Julie Bakke, The Menil Collection; Barbara Moore, Bound & Unbound; Antonia, Carmela, and Valentina Mulas, Archivio Ugo Mulas; Susan Kismaric, Jon Cordova, and Diane Farynyk,The Museum of Modern Art; Janis Ekdahl, The Museum of Modern Art Library; Edwin Lachnit and Barbara von der Heiden-Kopf, Museum of Modern Art Ludwig Foundation Vienna, formerly Hahn Collection, Cologne; Geoffrey Smith and Elva Griffith, Rare Books and Manuscripts, The Ohio State University Libraries; Gesine Tosin, Collection Onnasch; Harry Poster, Fairlawn, New Jersey; Luke Savisky, Austin; Shokus Video, Chatsworth, California; Jon Hendricks, The Gilbert and Lila Silverman Fluxus Collection; Connie Pleuckhahn, Sonitrol of Austin; Antonio Homen and Laura Bloom, Sonnabend Gallery, New York; Thomas Sokolowski, Geralyn Huxley, Andrea Wood, and Greg Pierce, The Andy Warhol Museum; Ron Platt, Will South, and Nora Kuper, Weatherspoon Art Gallery, The University of North Carolina at Greensboro; and Tim Wilkins, San Francisco.

This catalogue has its own team of contributors and collaborators: I thank Naomi Sawelson-Gorse for her essay studying the intersection between television programming and the visual arts during the early 1960s, which gives a unique picture of the values and mores of the era. For their help in facilitating the myriad details associated with the production of the catalogue, I wish to thank the following individuals and organizations: Valentina Balzarotti Barbieri, Agenzia Letteraria Internazionale, Milan; Karen Freedman, Alta Light Productions; Sarah Balcomb, Artists' Rights Society, New York; David Lombard, CBS Photo Archive, New York; Ron Rendon and Traci Goudie, 501 Post, Austin; Julie Greer, Houston; Leslie Wearb Hirsch, Art Collection, Harry Ransom Humanities Research Center, The University of Texas at Austin; Frances F. L. Beatty, Estate of Ray Johnson, New York; Nancy Reddin Kienholz; James Walsh, Meadowlane Enterprises, Inc., Van Nuys, California; Geraldine Aramanda, The Menil Collection; Thomas Grischkowsky, The Museum of Modern Art; Ulrike Müller, Museum of Modern Art Ludwig Foundation Vienna, formerly Hahn Collection, Cologne; Jane Klain, The Museum of Television & Radio, New York; Heidi Coleman, VAGA, New York; Joan Rothfuss and Heather Thimm, Walker Art Center, Minneapolis; Lisa Miriello, The Andy Warhol Museum; and Eileen Adele Hale, Estate of Garry Winogrand, Los Angeles.

My thanks also go to Alan Shaffer in Venice, California, and Jeff Rowe of Austin Prints for Publication, who provided photographs of works by Wallace Berman, Dennis Hopper, and Nam June Paik for this catalogue. Robyn Ross proofread the manuscript with great precision and care. Catalogue designer Russell Hassell's masterful design abilities are evident on each page of this publication. As always, I am grateful to Russell for his unerring aesthetic advice.

The staff of the Austin Museum of Art has worked with great dedication in coordinating all aspects of the exhibition, and I offer them immense thanks for the skill and ingenuity they have demonstrated in bringing it to fruition: Dana Friis-Hansen, Chief Curator, was invaluable in securing key loans to the exhibition and supervising its installation in Austin. Lisa Dirks, Publications Coordinator, edited this catalogue with meticulous care, working countless hours to assure a publication of the highest possible standards. Her professionalism and good humor proved to be valuable traits during the development of this complex book. In addition, Gail Sanders, Curatorial Coordinator, worked for two years in the coordination of loans from throughout Europe and the United States and assisted with catalogue production; Gail is also to be commended for undertaking a range of challenging duties with grace and skill. Erica Shamaly, Exhibitions Associate, was instrumental in researching and obtaining videos and audiovisual equipment for the exhibition and in providing artists' biographical information; Joe Janson, Preparator, and Bill Nichols, Assistant Preparator, and their crew carried out the installation of the exhibition with their customary professionalism. Exhibition Intern Gillian Born Elliot's fact-checking skills and expertise in German were valuable contributions to the catalogue. Todd Sandel, Membership Assistant, offered his much needed and much appreciated assistance with proofreading the manuscript. Many others worked behind the scenes in the departments for Administration, Development, and Education to make this exhibition possible.

I wish to express our deepest gratitude to the underwriters of *The New Frontier: Art and Television, 1960–65*. The AT&T Foundation and its Austin representative, Vincent J. Salas, have been most generous in their support of the exhibition. I wish also to thank Arthur Frakes for his vital commitment to this project.

Finally, I am grateful to the Austin Museum of Art's Board of Trustees for its support and commitment to presenting significant and challenging exhibitions to our Central Texas audience. *The New Frontier* represents the type of ambitious exhibitions we plan to present in our new permanent building, scheduled to open in downtown Austin in 2003.

Elizabeth Ferrer
The Dr. and Mrs. Ernest C. Butler Executive Director

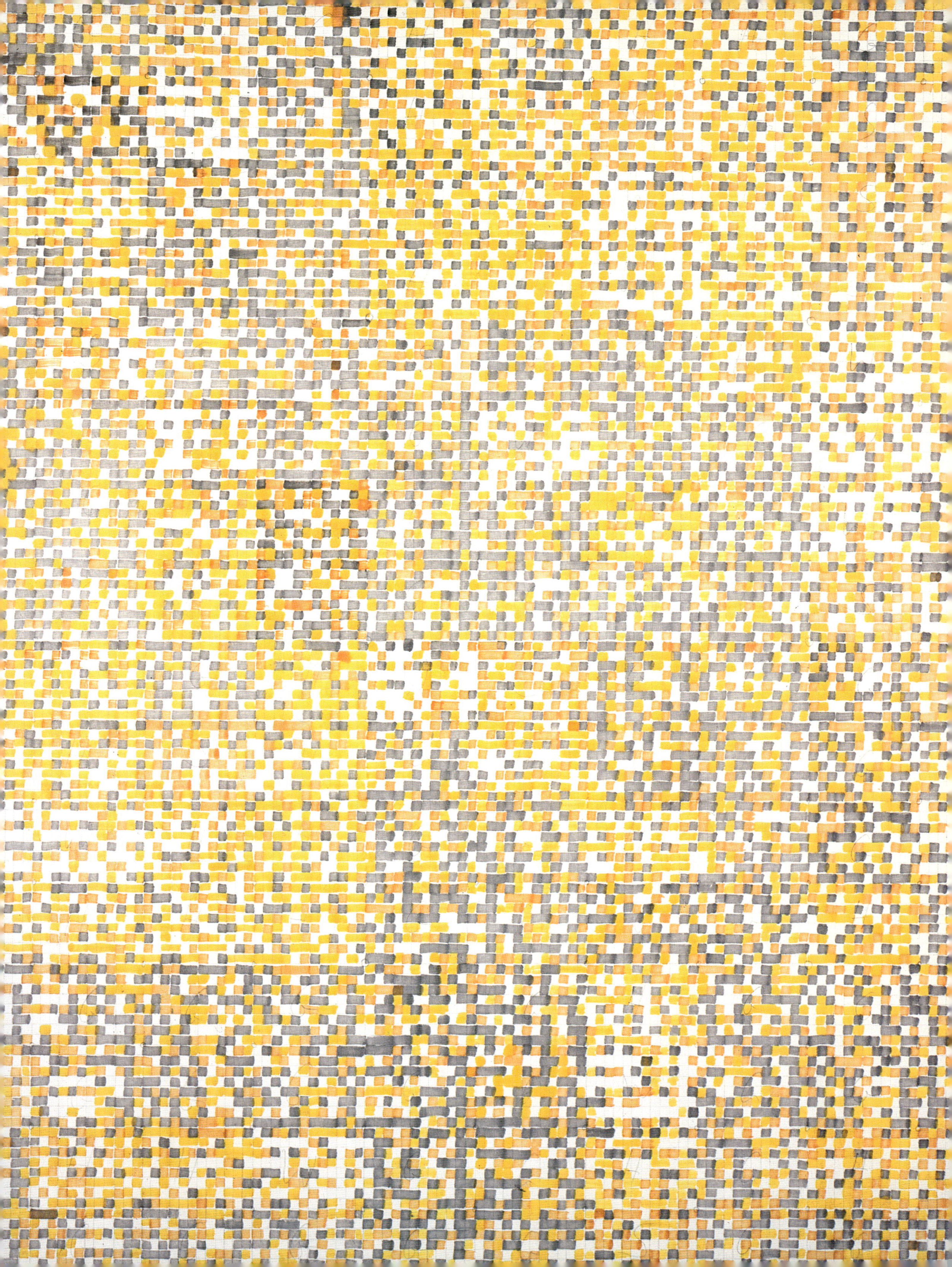

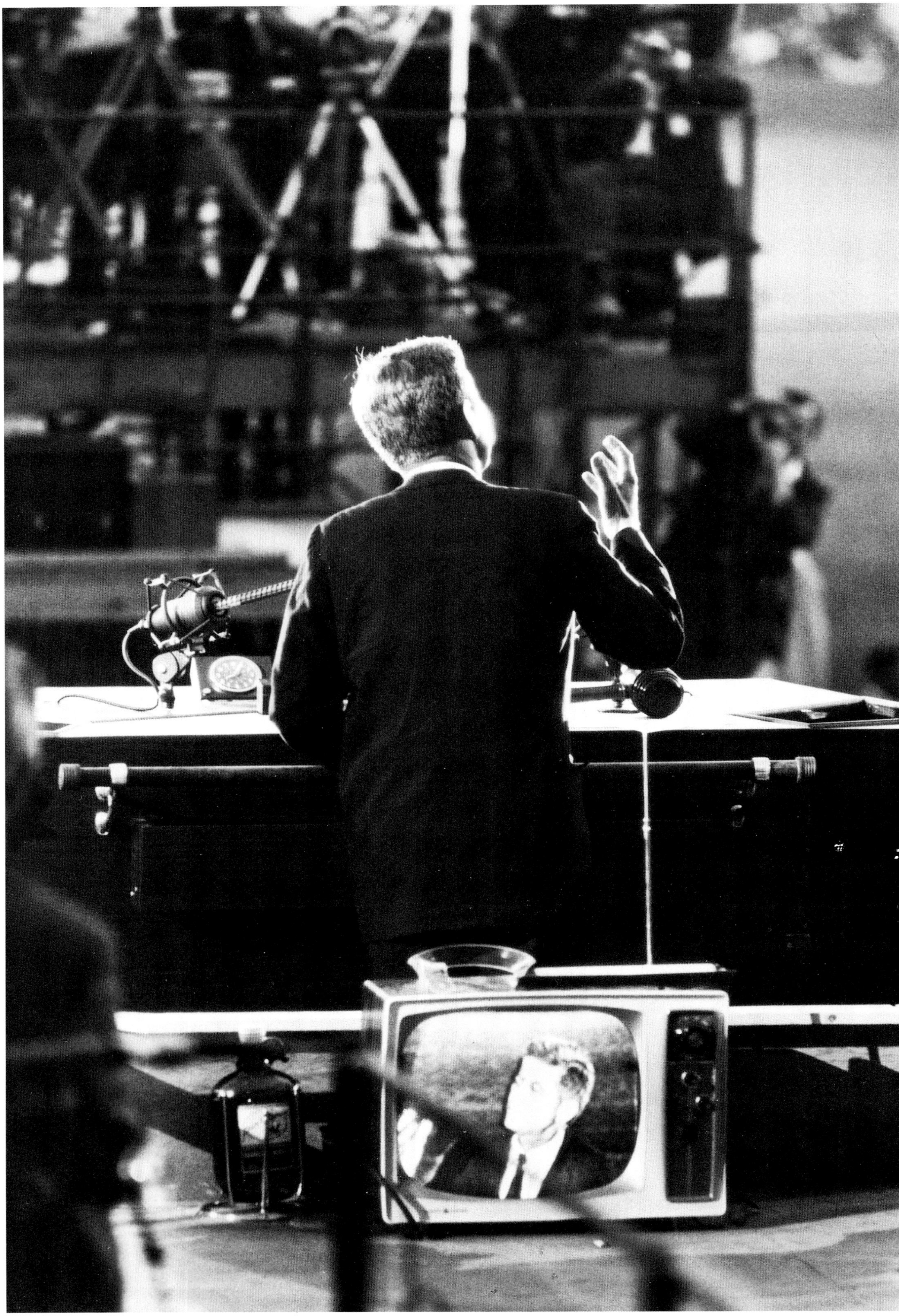

Pop People

JOHN ALAN FARMER

On July 15, 1960, Garry Winogrand photographed John F. Kennedy at the Democratic National Convention in Los Angeles as he accepted his party's nomination as its presidential candidate.[1] In Winogrand's photograph, a television set relaying a live broadcast of the speech sits on a table behind Kennedy—an emblematic image of a man who would soon be christened by journalists as the "Television President," in recognition of his masterful use of the medium. In his acceptance speech, Kennedy stated that "we stand today on the edge of a New Frontier—the frontier of the 1960s. . . . Beyond that frontier are the uncharted areas of space and science, unsolved problems of peace and war, unconquered pockets of ignorance and prejudice, unanswered questions of poverty and surplus. . . . But I believe the times demand new invention, innovation, imagination, decision. I am asking each of you to be pioneers on that New Frontier."[2] Kennedy well understood that by the beginning of the 1960s, television had become the primary technology for the production, distribution, and consumption of images, and during his administration, television emerged as an indelible feature on the landscape of The New Frontier.

The dominance of the photographic and filmic image was giving way to a technology in which images were produced by the phosphorescence of electronic signals transmitted simultaneously by electromagnetic waves or coaxial cables from a sender to multiple receivers in real time, effectively integrating sender and receiver into a circuit. The major televisual spectacles of the first half of the decade, ranging from the Nixon-Kennedy debates of September 1960, to the first transcontinental broadcast by *Telstar I* in July 1962, to the assassination of Kennedy and its aftermath in November 1963, illustrated the extent to which this circuit was in effect a vast network of consumers and producers linked electronically via images. Through these images, fluid structures of power, systems of truth, and strategies of desire were continuously shaped, reshaped, and integrated seamlessly into the rhythms of everyday

GARRY WINOGRAND

Democratic National Convention,
Los Angeles, 1960
Gelatin silver print
20 × 16 inches (51 × 41 cm)
Courtesy Fraenkel Gallery, San Francisco

life. Television's rising cultural authority during this pivotal period resided in its capacity to legitimate the new modes of perception, consciousness, and behavior it was putting in place. And in the work of the artists who engaged with this medium at this time, the effects of television's reconfiguration of the relationship between image and reality were emerging in a variety of artistic media, including painting, sculpture, performance, and intermedia.

Television as a Cultural Form

In his best-selling book *Understanding Media: The Extensions of Man*, first published in 1963, the cultural critic Marshall McLuhan explored in detail the physical, psychic, and social effects of what he called the passage from mechanical to electronic culture—a passage accelerated by the invention and dissemination of television. In the 1960s, his formulation of this transition had a tremendous influence on popular conceptions of television not only as a technology, but also as a cultural form. McLuhan argued that while mechanical technologies extended the physical capacities of specific parts of the body, the electronic media, beginning with the telegraph, extended the central nervous system. Television, he asserted, was the most momentous of the new electronic technologies because it was "the most recent and spectacular electric extension of our central nervous system."[3]

In "Television: The Timid Giant," the chapter devoted to his analysis of the medium, McLuhan stated that television's primary cultural impact is a function of its intrinsic properties as a medium, rather than of the content of specific programs. In contrast to the high-resolution mediums of photography and film, television extends the senses with a relatively low degree of sensory information. As he wrote, "The TV image is not a *still* shot. It is not a photo in any sense, but a ceaselessly forming contour of things limned by the scanning-finger. The resulting plastic contour appears by light through, not light on, and the image so formed has the quality of sculpture and icon, rather than of picture." He continued: "The TV image requires each instant that we 'close' the spaces in the mesh by a convulsive sensuous participation that is profoundly kinetic and tactile, because tactility is the interplay of the senses, rather than the isolated contact of skin and object."[4] By placing the televisual image in the category of sculpture rather than painting, McLuhan attempted to underscore what he termed the "tactile properties" of the medium. The televisual image acquires a para-material presence that practically

Nixon-Kennedy debate
of September 1960.
(not included in this exhibition)

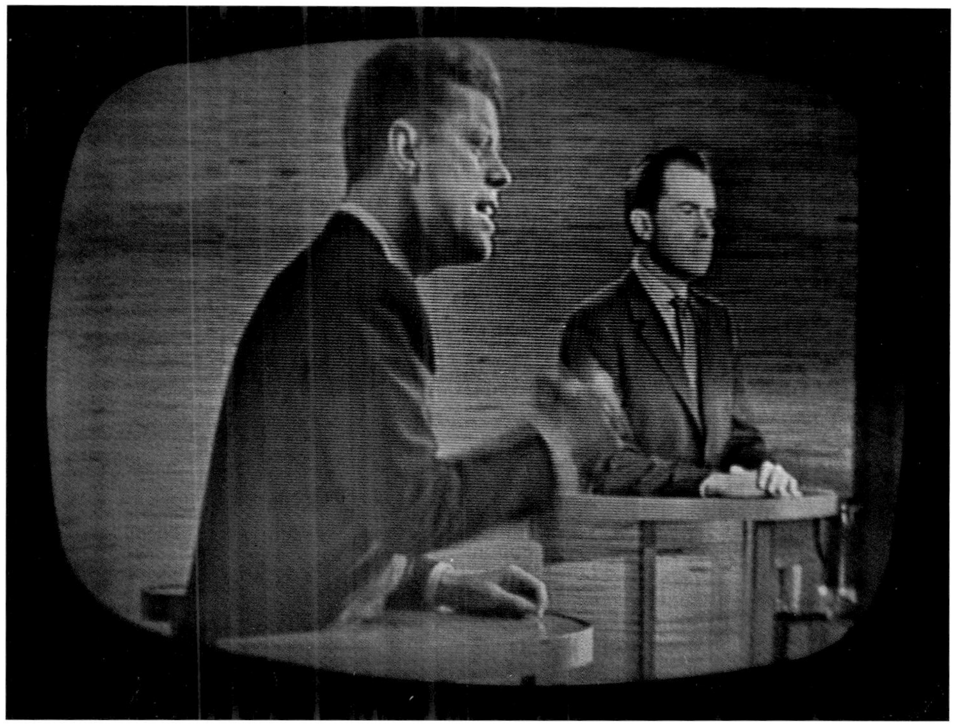

enables it to be touched. It produces a liminal zone in which common-sense distinctions between bodies and images are redefined.

For McLuhan, artists played a crucial role in detecting the physical, psychic, and social transformations wrought by the growing dominance of electronic mediums such as television—changes that become apparent to the general public only after such technologies have become firmly ensconced. "The effects of technology do not occur at the level of opinions or concepts, but alter sense ratios or patterns of perception steadily and without resistance," he asserted. "The serious artist is the only person able to encounter technology with impunity just because he is an expert aware of the changes in sense perception."[5] He isolated the painter Paul Cézanne in particular, who was working when the first electronic technologies were being introduced in the late nineteenth century. As McLuhan wrote, "It is not hard to explain this revolution to painters and sculptors, for they have been striving, ever since Cézanne abandoned perspective illusion in favor of structure in painting, to bring about the very change that TV has now effected on a fantastic scale. . . . The aggressive lunge of artistic strategy for the remaking of Western man has, via TV, become a vulgar sprawl and an overwhelming splurge in American life."[6] In addition to Cézanne, McLuhan also cited other modernist artists as forecasters of the visual effects inherent in television. These included Georges Seurat, who produced representational images with dots of paint (anticipating television's formation of images from pixels of light), and Georges Rouault, who evoked the effect of light shining through glass in many of his works (anticipating the formation of the televisual images from light shining from behind, rather than projected onto, a screen). Lending support to McLuhan's assertion that artists are especially receptive to the effects of new technologies before they become apparent to the public at large, in the late 1950s and early 1960s artists associated with the so-called Neo-Dada avant-garde began to produce a plethora of works that registered television's transformative impact on the experience of social reality.

The Neo-Dada Avant-Garde and Television

The Neo-Dada avant-garde, which embraced a variety of tendencies, ranging from Pop to Fluxus to Assemblage, sought to explore ways of reconnecting art and life by looking to the precedent of Dada and other avant-garde movements of the early twentieth century.[7] As a result of their reception of Dada, the Neo-Dadaists absorbed and transformed key strategies by which avant-garde artists had used mass-media imaging technologies to reconnect art and life—including photomontage, filmic montage, the readymade, and the staging of actions that incorporated the mass media.[8] Through these strategies, exponents of both the historical avant-gardes and the neo-avant-gardes attempted to critique, reform, and sometimes destroy the dominant social order by exploiting what they perceived to be the emancipatory potential of imaging technologies. These technologies, many artists insisted, had the potential to open up new ways of seeing that could catalyze the development of a revolutionary consciousness and transform social reality.

Nevertheless, the reception of Dada ideas and influences in the United States and Western Europe in the late 1950s and early 1960s took place during a period in which the configurations of technological, social, and economic relations were vastly different from those operating in Berlin, New York, or Zürich in the 1910s and 1920s. If imaging technologies were, indeed, one of the means by which Dada artists sought to reconnect art and life, they had changed radically since the post–World War I era. In contrast to magazines, newspapers, photography, and film, television was an electronic medium, and the televisual image possessed a more technologically mediated relationship to reality than the photographic or filmic image did. Yet, in spite of the low definition of the televisual image, television's mimetic quality, its liveness, and the fact that it was integrated into the rhythms of the individual's daily domestic life invested it with great power. Governments and corporations, the institutions that controlled the production and transmission of television programming, exploited this authority to shape viewers' consciousness of themselves as citizens and consumers. In this regard, the ideological content of programs and commercials, as well as the normalization of a mode of passive viewing that made audiences more receptive to these ideologies, were equally important.

Some Neo-Dada artists, such as Nam June Paik and Wolf Vostell, sought through their work to make viewers conscious of what they regarded as the oppressive model of viewing embodied by the passive practice of watching television, though the artistic strategies they developed were not aligned with revolutionary politics as rigorously as those of the Dada and Soviet Constructivist/Productivist avant-gardes. The attempts of other Neo-Dada artists, such as Robert Rauschenberg and Andy Warhol, to reconnect art and life by engaging with the mass media were not motivated by revolutionary politics at all. If the concept of a utopia catalyzed by technology was still sustainable in the post–World War II era, it was the utopia formulated not by Marxist philosophy, but by figures such as McLuhan, who anticipated the emergence of a "global village" linked together in harmony through electronic mediums of communication such as television.

Isolated artists in the United States and Western Europe began to engage with television, whether consciously or not, in the years immediately following World War II; this number had expanded greatly by the late 1950s. During this decade, television became available to virtually the entire population of these regions, and the critical reception of Dada made many artists more receptive to the mass media than had been the case with the preceding artistic generation of Abstract Expressionists, whose focus on abstraction had tended to preclude a close engagement with radio, television, or film. In the United States, most of these artists lived or worked in New York or Los Angeles, the two most important centers of both art and television production at the time; in Western Europe, most lived or worked in West Germany.

The new frontier that these artists engaged with was that of the Pop Person, as Andy Warhol stated in an article published in the May 23, 1966, issue of the *San Francisco Chronicle*; a person who consumes images voraciously and "is made up from what he's seen. Television has done it. You don't have to read anymore. Books will go

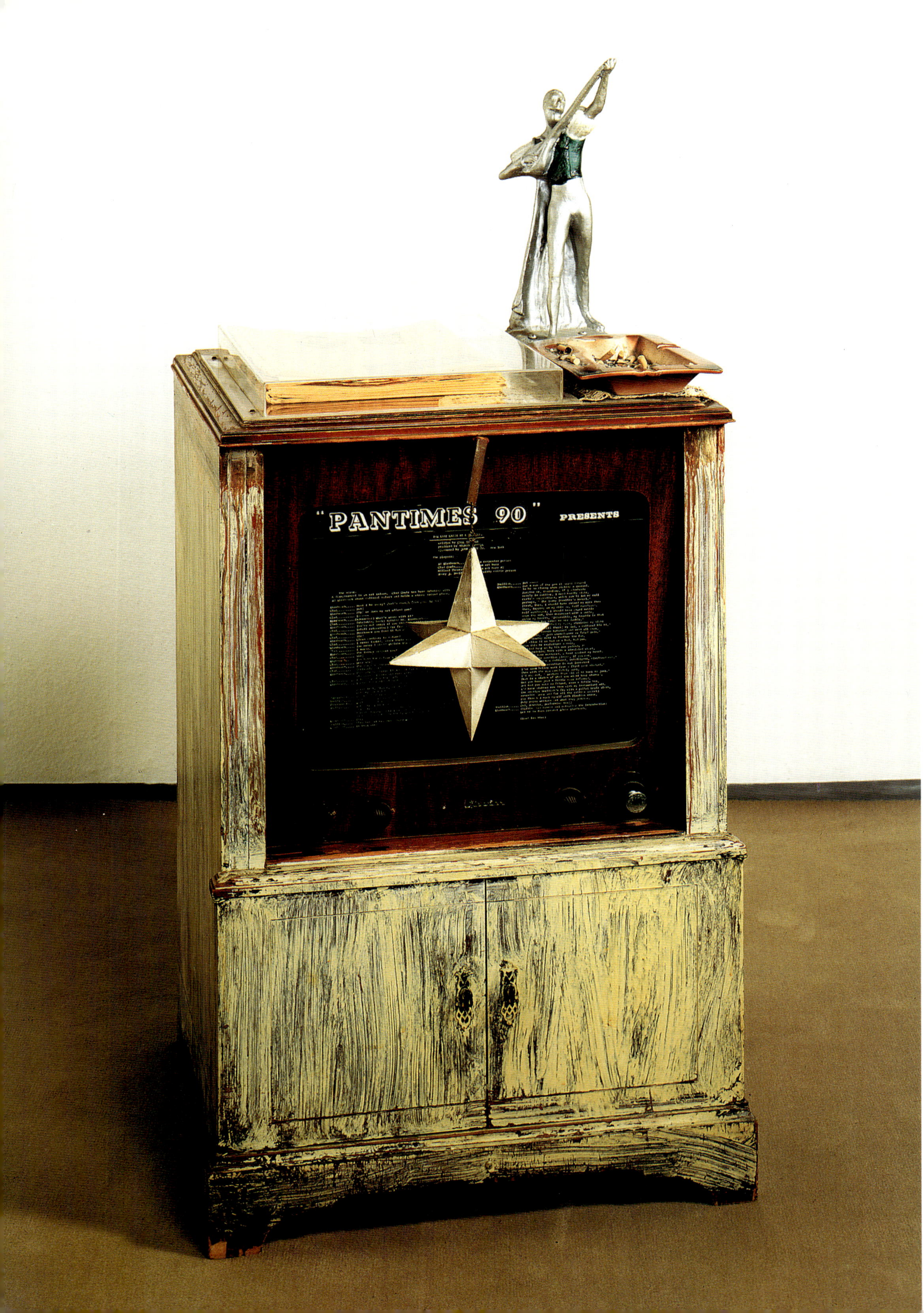
"PANTIMES 90" PRESENTS

EDWARD KIENHOLZ

The Big Eye (Homage to H.S.), 1961
Painted television console, plastic, newspaper, and figurine
56 × 24 × 30 inches
(142 × 61 × 76 cm)
Collection Onnasch, Berlin

out, television will stay. Movies will go out, television will stay. And that is why people are really becoming plastic; they are just fed things and formed and the people who can give things back are considered very talented."[9] As the Pop Person began to absorb the images transmitted to him or her through television, the distinction between the television world and the real world became increasingly ambiguous. Social reality approached the "hyperreality" that the philosopher Jean Baudrillard has described, in which the real implodes into its representation and in which the individual is exposed to more and more sophisticated systems of control that render emancipation from this order increasingly improbable. Artists at the dawn of this new frontier, in the name of reconnecting art and life in the tradition of their avant-garde predecessors, played a crucial role in the emergence of this world, whether by passively affirming it or by actively contesting it.

TV Land

In 1961, Edward Kienholz produced a work titled *The Big Eye (Homage to H.S.)*, the first of a series of works he would produce during this decade using the body of an actual television set. Inspired by a negative review of one of his exhibitions by the critic Henry Seldis, the work consists of the chassis of a television set, on whose screen is printed an adaptation of Cyrano de Bergerac's monologue on the art of insulting others; the white star that hangs in front of the screen is meant to evoke the logo of the popular dramatic series, *Playhouse 90*.[10]

Kienholz was one of the first artists to use the television set, which had begun to assume an increasingly prominent role in the homes of middle-class families in the United States and Western Europe, as the structure for a work of art. In many families, the television set was displayed proudly in the living room, usurping the place of the radio, the piano, and other sources of entertainment. Moreover, as the cultural historian Lynn Spigel observes in *Make Room for TV: Television and the Family Ideal in Postwar America*, the television set was often anthropomorphized as "a member of the family," "a family friend," "a nurse," "a teacher," and even "a family pet."[11] While this anthropomorphization served to assuage the public's anxieties about an unfamiliar object by familiarizing it, the substitution of the television set for the human being also symbolized a shift in the experience of social reality: increasingly, the electronic images broadcast on television were invested with the material authority of reality, which was in turn dissolved into the medium of television, embodied by the box in the living room.

LEE FRIEDLANDER

Washington, D.C., 1962
Gelatin silver print
14 × 11 inches (36 × 28 cm)
Courtesy Fraenkel Gallery, San Francisco

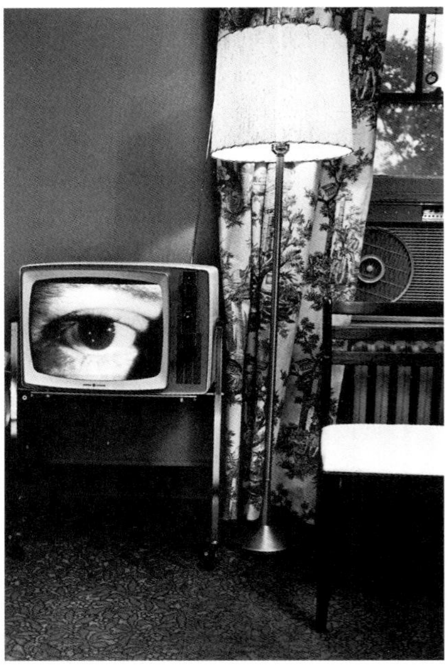

In 1961, Lee Friedlander began a series of black-and-white photographs of television sets in interiors in which the only human beings are the low-definition images of the men, women, and children on the screens. In these "Deft, witty, spanking little poems of hate," as the photographer Walker Evans described them when they were first reproduced in *Harper's Bazaar* in 1963, Friedlander pictured the television set not as a member of the family, but as an ominous intruder. Perhaps most frightening are the sets that feature close-ups of individual faces or parts of faces, such as eyes. In these photographs, which evoke scenes from 1950s science-fiction films and foreshadow the 1980s classic *Videodrome*, it is almost as if the sets represent a new type of human being, whose physical body has been dematerialized into the flux of electromagnetic transmission and is contained in a chassis, from which it monitors those still yoked by the burden of physical bodies.

For many artists, television served as a means through which life entered the rarefied space of the artist's studio to produce an ambient environment of light and sound that mediated their relationship with reality. For example, television was an integral presence in the ambient environment in which Robert Rauschenberg conceived and produced his silkscreen paintings. In response to a query from the art critic Barbara Rose about why he began in the late 1950s to create works by printing, instead of drawing, images, Rauschenberg replied: "I don't want my personality to come out through the piece. That's why I keep television on all the time. And I keep the windows open. I want my paintings to be reflections of life, and life can't be stopped."[12] In contrast to many artists and critics of the Abstract Expressionist generation, who perceived the work of art as an index of the artist's physical, psychological, and even spiritual presence, Rauschenberg declared that he aspired to make work in which the self is subsumed into the totality of existence—into what he called "life." Moreover, he connected life with television—an identification he underscored by linking the turned-on television set with open windows. In this manner he rhetorically ascribed to the stream of televisual information the status of the real world outside his window. The distinction between the televisual and the material world became even more blurred when Rauschenberg permitted a television crew to film him producing *Barge* (1962–63), his largest silkscreen painting, for an interview with Mike Wallace that was broadcast on CBS. If only temporarily, the artist's studio became a television studio; the artist, a performer; and the process of artistic production, a media event.

Andy Warhol also often worked with the television set turned on. From the time he bought his first set in the late 1950s, Warhol anthropomorphized the television

LEE FRIEDLANDER

Florida, 1963
Gelatin silver print
11 × 14 inches (28 × 36 cm)
Courtesy Fraenkel Gallery, San Francisco

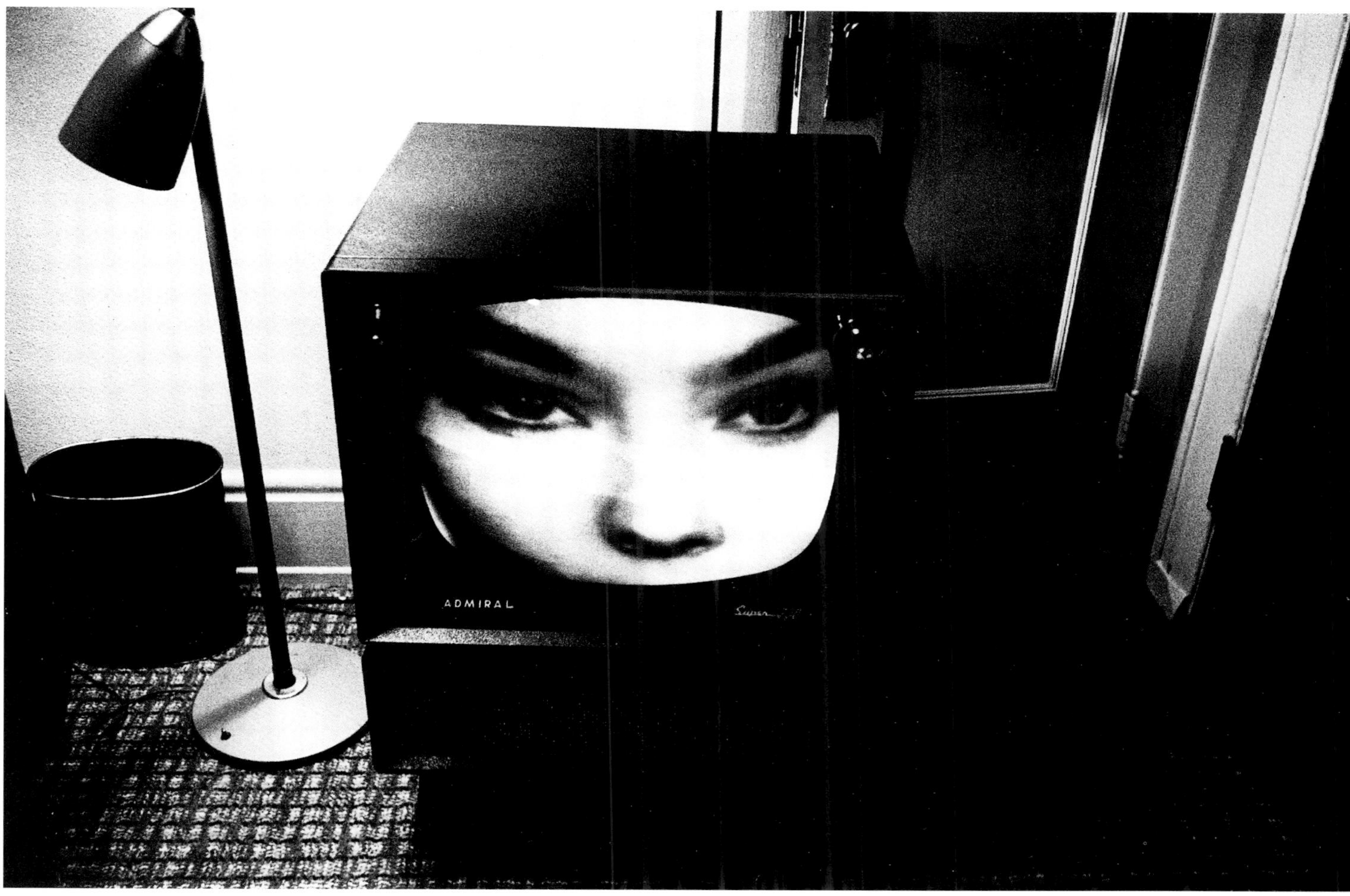

LEE FRIEDLANDER

Philadelphia, 1961
Gelatin silver print
11 × 14 inches (28 × 36 cm)
Courtesy Fraenkel Gallery, San Francisco

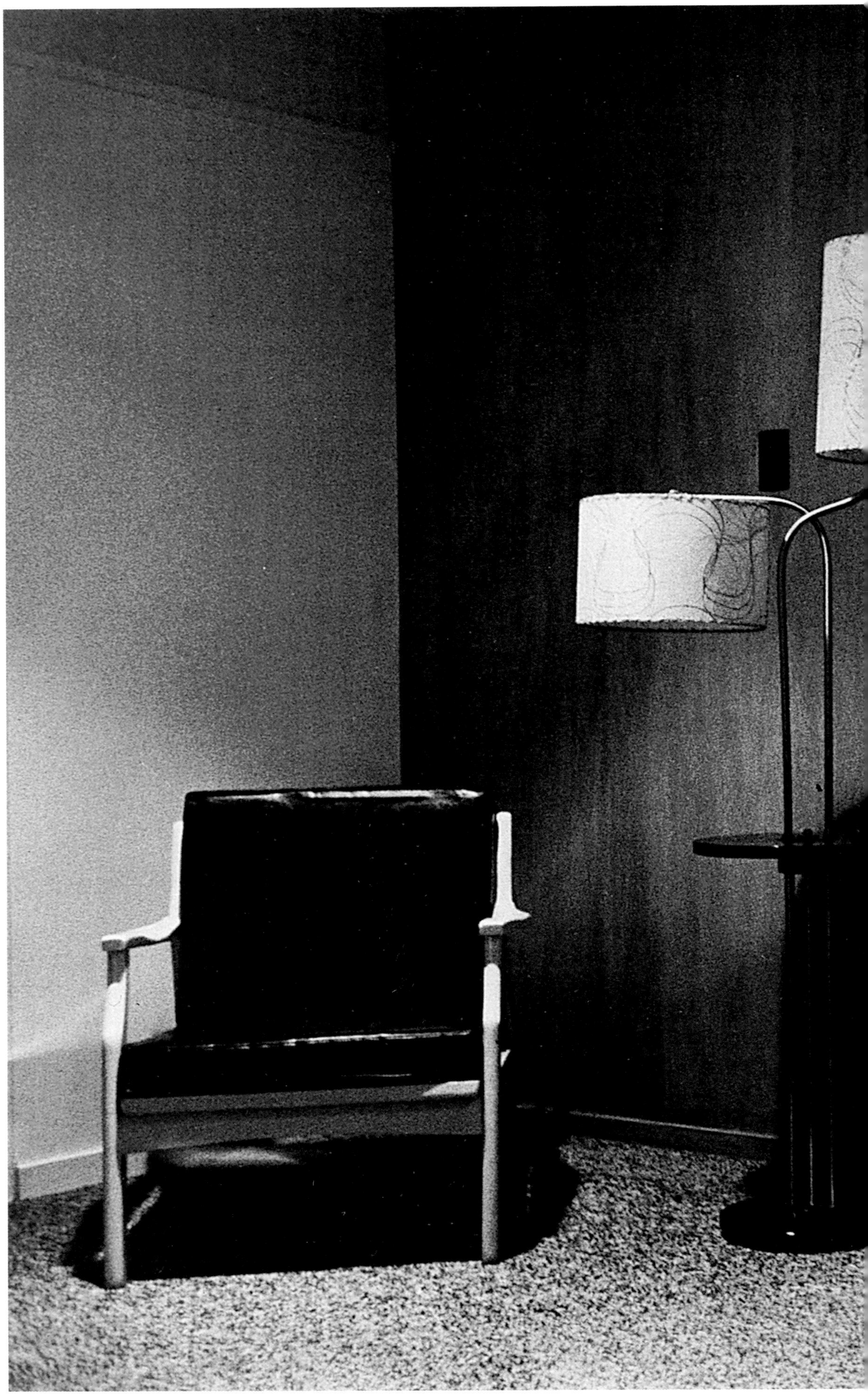

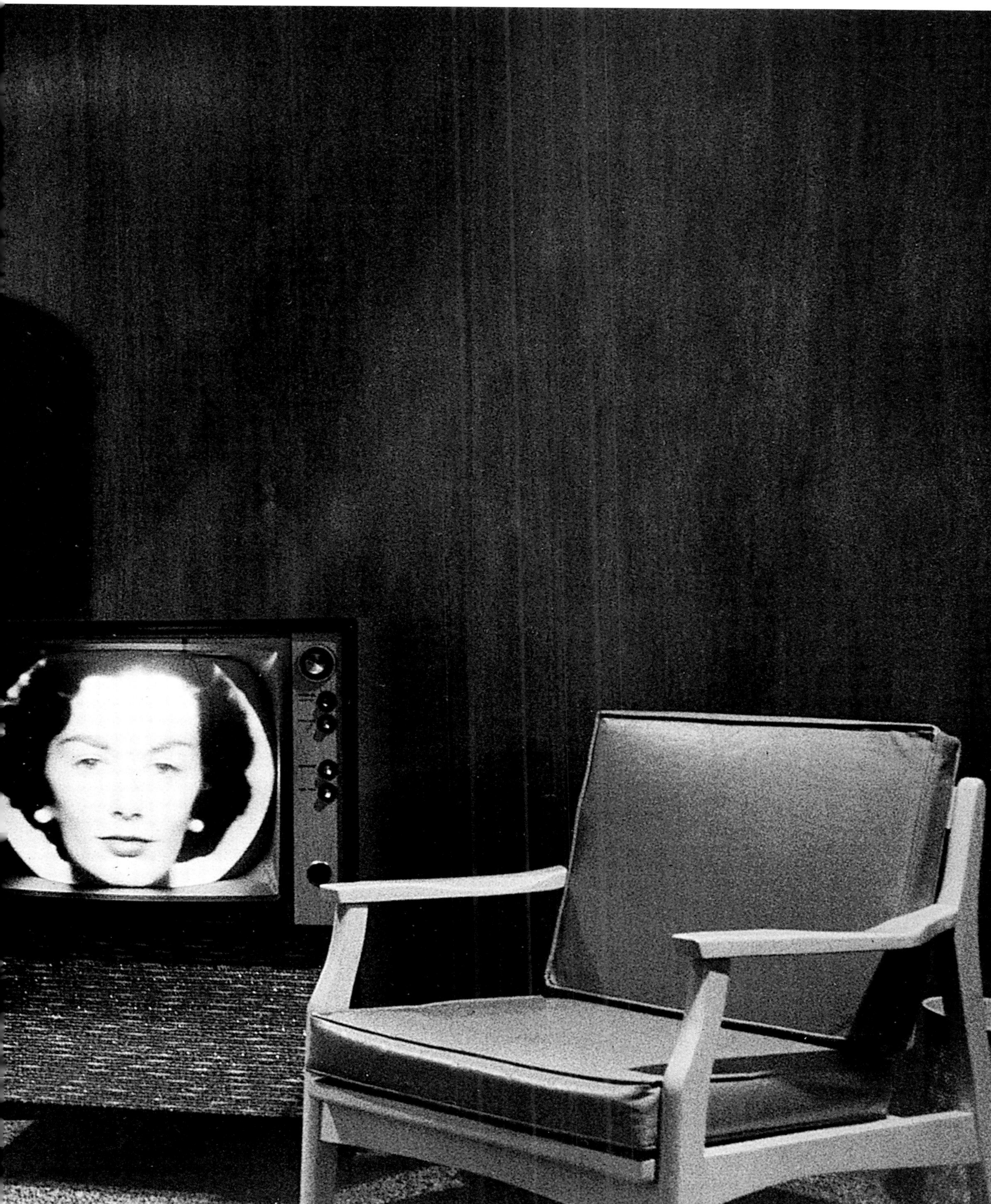

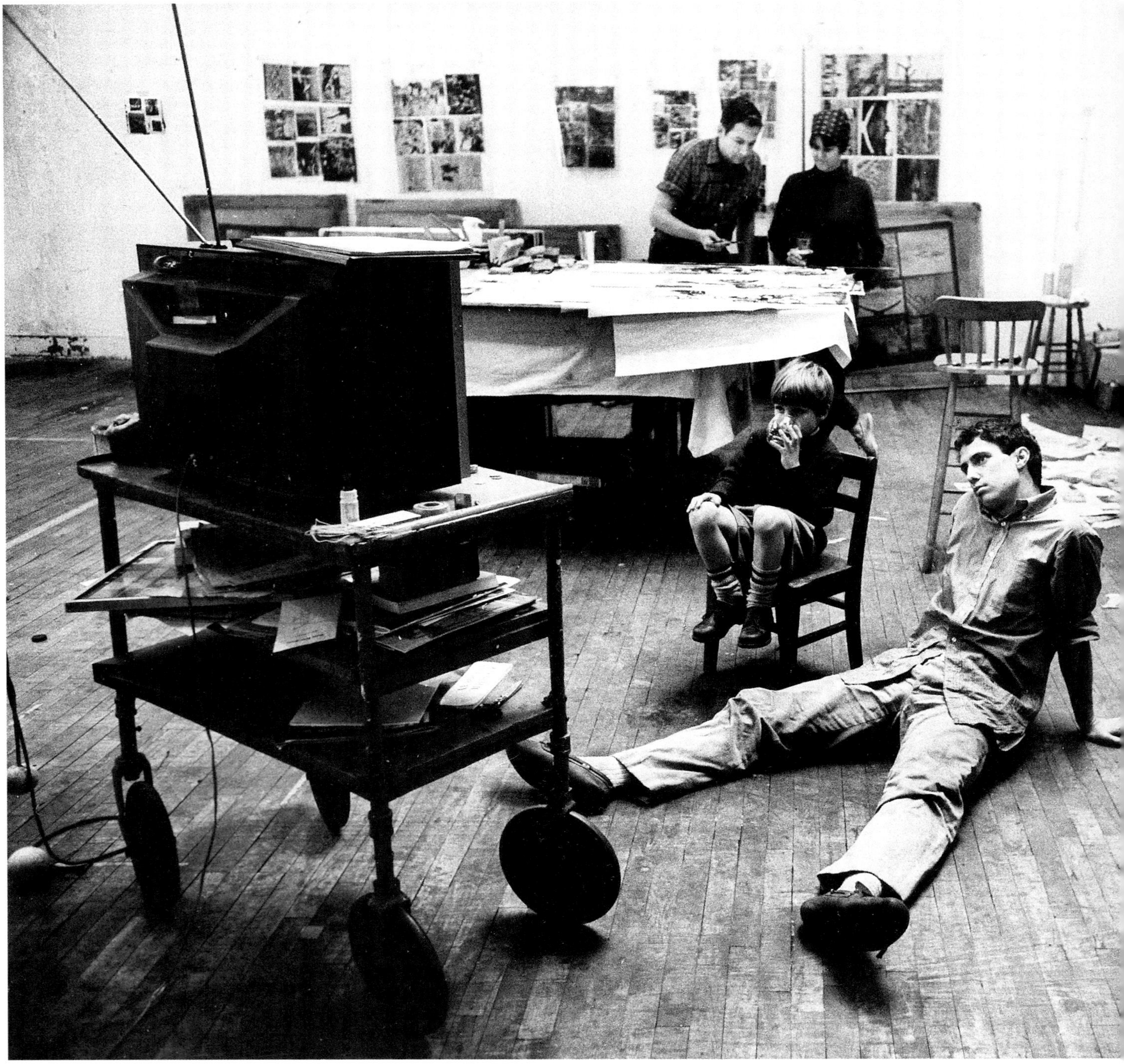

UGO MULAS

Untitled (Robert Rauschenberg
with Elaine Sturtevant in his studio
in New York City, while Steve
Paxton and Rauschenberg's son,
Christopher, watch television), 1965
Gelatin silver print
11 × 15 inches (28 × 39 cm)
Archivio Ugo Mulas, Milan

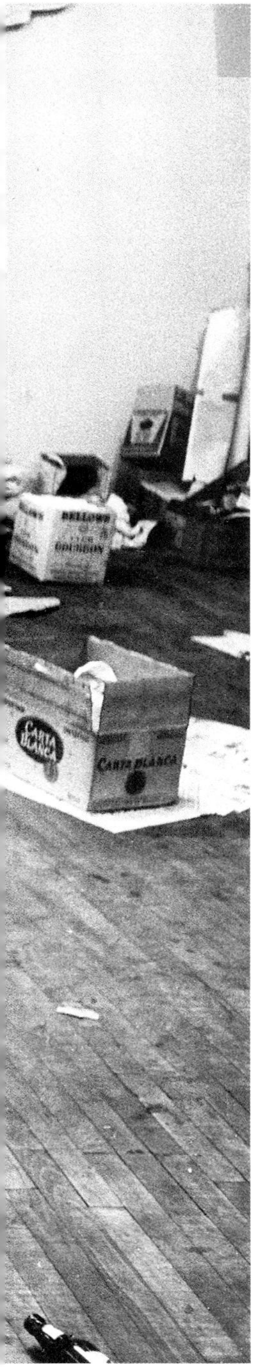

set as a surrogate companion that replaced the necessity of interacting with other human beings all the time. As he once wrote, "When I got my first TV set, I stopped caring so much about close relationships with other people. I'd been hurt a lot to the degree you can only be hurt if you care a lot. So I guess I did care a lot. . . . So in the late 50s I started an affair with my television which has continued to the present, when I play around in my bedroom with as many as four at a time. But I didn't get married until 1964 when I got my first tape recorder. My wife."[13] To Warhol, the television set, as well as the tape recorder, became an intimate companion whose seductive presence replaced the necessity for human relationships. His assertion of his "affair" with television underscores the almost sexual aspect of this bond, as does the fact that he placed no fewer than four sets in his bedroom.

Screens

In the late 1950s and early 1960s, many artists began to register the emergence of the new perceptual modality signified by television by inventing pictorial spaces that no longer functioned in terms of traditional Western models of picture-making. In the Renaissance, the pictorial surface was conceived as a window onto an imaginary space that was rendered continuous with the viewer's space through the use of linear perspective. In the Baroque period, especially in Northern Europe, the pictorial surface was conceived as a mirror of optical reality. In the twentieth century, some artists began to explore the flatness of the pictorial surface in purely abstract terms, without reference to the material world. But beginning in the 1950s, many artists began to conceive the pictorial surface as a screen—a tendency reflected in the work of those who adopted new modes of painting (such as silkscreen), experimented with the collage aesthetic, and incorporated actual television sets into works of art.

In 1958, Wolf Vostell produced a work entitled *TV-dé-coll/age, No. 1*, which vandalized the mediums of both modernist painting and popular television. This work consists of six television sets, set to broadcast static, placed behind a monochromatic canvas lacerated in six places, so that the static is visible behind the slashes. This strategy differed considerably from the elegantly sliced monochrome canvases of Lucio Fontana's *Tagli* series, also begun in 1958. It was a stunning purity of surface, and a dark, existential void revealed by delicate incisions, that this High Modernist sought. The wounds Vostell inflicted onto the pictorial surface reveal

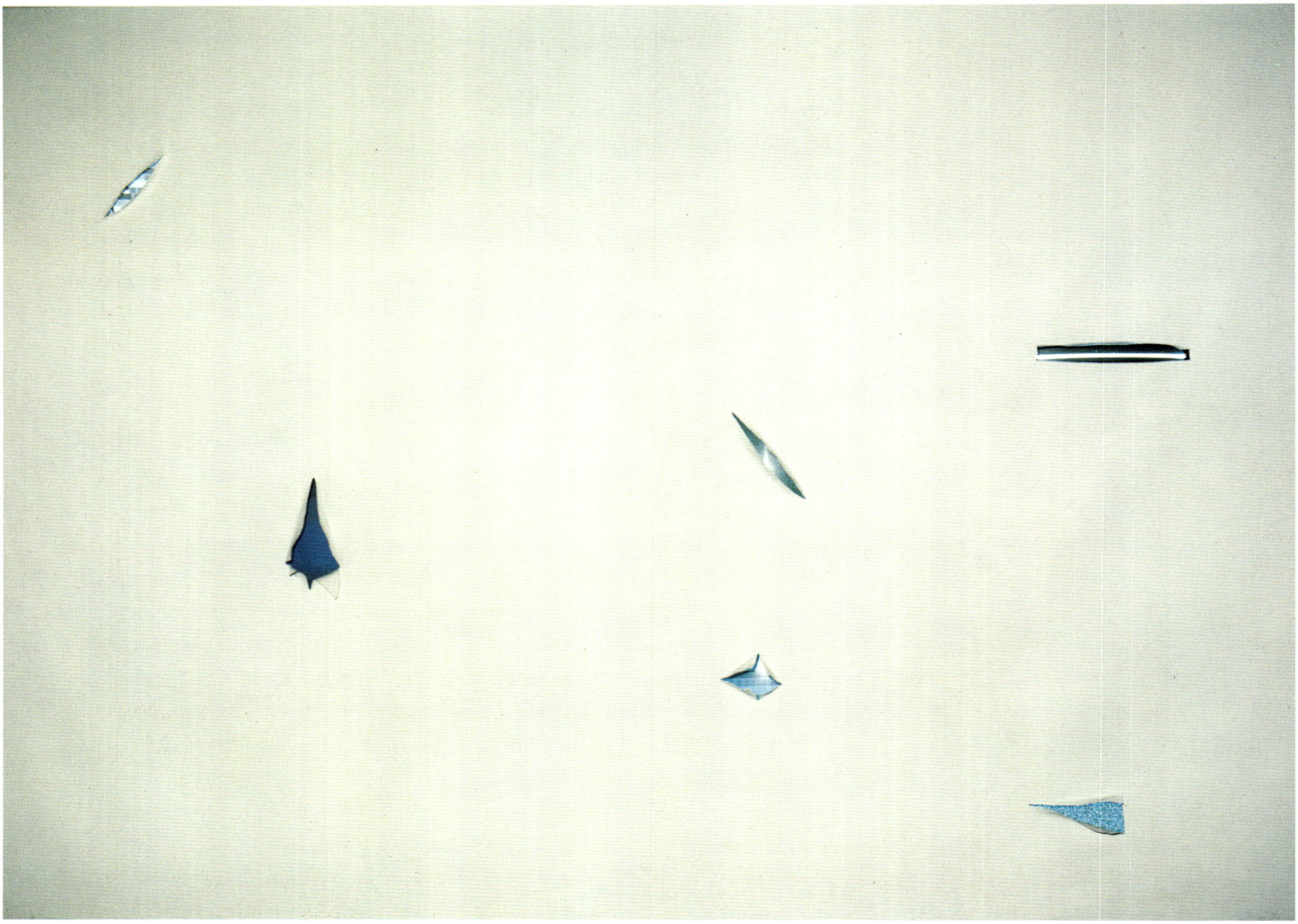

WOLF VOSTELL

TV-dé-coll/age, No. 1, 1958–59
Six television sets behind canvas
99 × 134 × 32 inches (250 × 340 × 80 cm)
Courtesy Fine Art Rafael Vostell, Berlin

K. O. GÖTZ

Statistisch-metrische Modulation 12:2:1, 1960
Felt pen on cardboard
20 × 26 inches (50 × 65 cm)
Collection of the artist

Statistisch-metrische Modulation 12:3:1, 1960
Felt pen on cardboard
20 × 26 inches (50 × 65 cm)
Collection of the artist

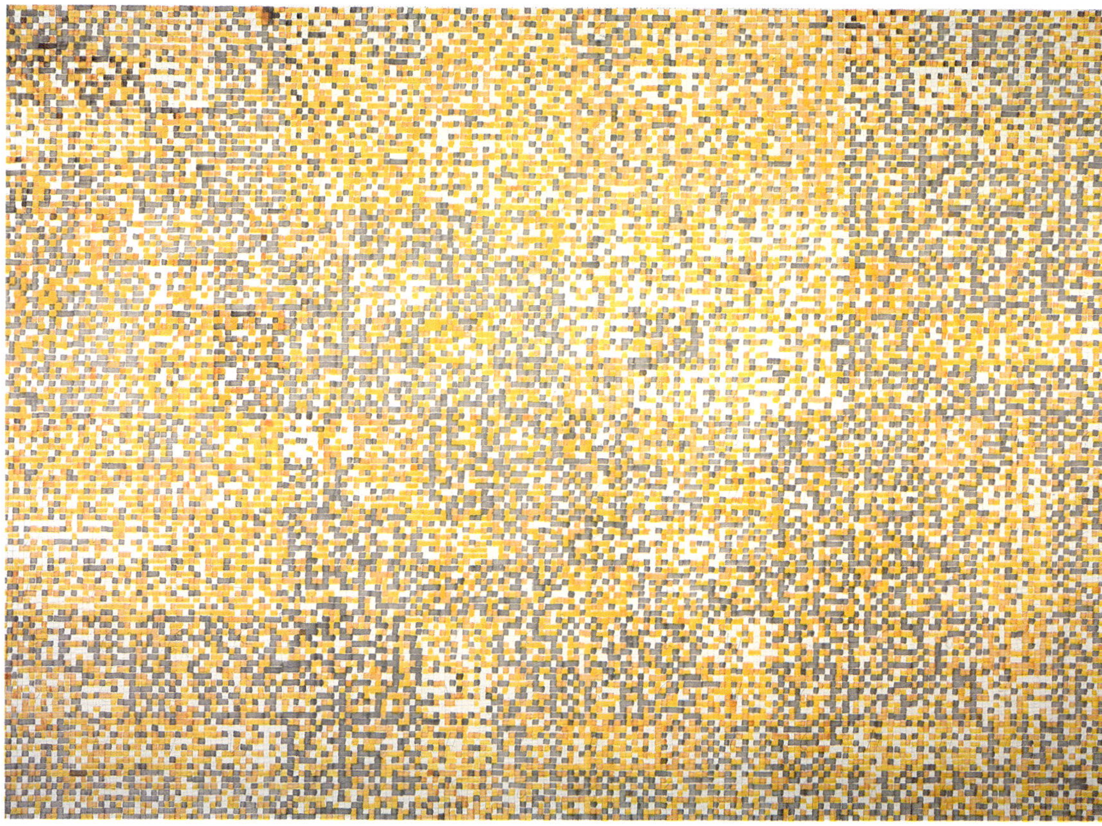

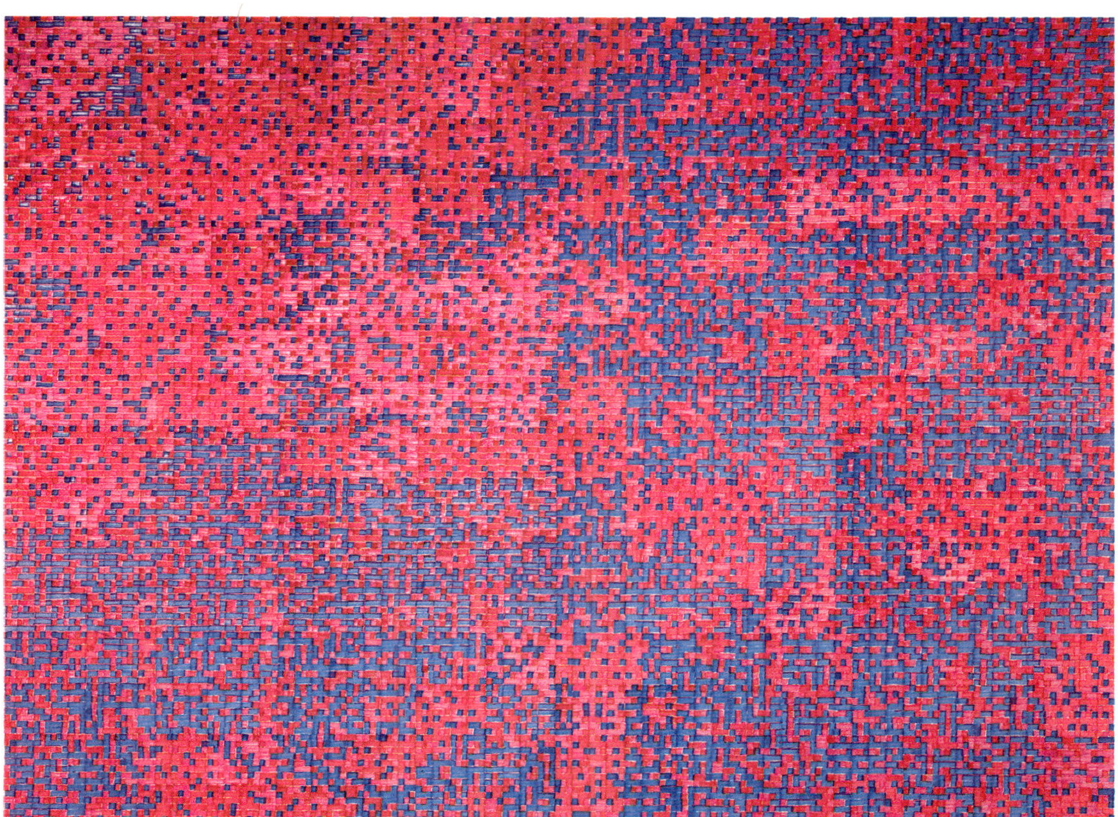

K. O. GÖTZ

Density 10:3:2:1, 1960
Felt pen on cardboard on canvas
79 × 108 inches (200 × 260 cm)
Collection of the artist

behind an abstract painting yet another "abstract painting," rendered poetically not in paint but in flickering pixels of black and white. The fact that the static bleeds through the lacerated surface of the canvas symbolically suggests the degree to which the mass media in general, and television in particular, have come to mediate the perception of modernist painting and the model of contemplative viewing it attempted to foster.

A year after Vostell produced *TV-dé-coll/age, No. 1*, K. O. Götz began a series of paintings on panels entitled *Rasterbilder* (Raster Pictures), a term that refers to the grid of pixels into which a television screen is divided, which contaminated the purity of modernist painting in another way. These works derived from Götz's attempts to develop his concept of *Elektronische Malerei* (Electronic Painting)—a contemporary aesthetic inspired by the most advanced electronic technologies—that would break with classical painting by investing the works with both a spatial and a temporal dimension, in which form exists in a perpetual state of becoming.

In the *Rasterbilder*, the pictorial surface is conceived as if it were a screen divided into thousands of pixels arranged in a grid. Götz would arbitrarily select a ratio defining the relationships among four different levels of brightness and would then subdivide the grid into smaller and smaller grids according to this ratio, until he was ultimately able to determine the level of luminosity of each individual pixel. In the early 1960s, he produced many of his *Rasterbilder* in collaboration with Karin Martin, one of his students, and even produced a *Rasterfilm* entitled *Density 10:2:2:1* (1962), a *Rasterbild* in motion. In addition to reflecting his interest in computer programming, the process by which Götz and his student created these works also reveals his interest in how the televisual image is produced. Like such images, Götz's *Rasterbilder* are the products of a technologically derived aesthetic in which visual representation becomes a function of the translation of information into a code. In fact, the *Rasterbilder* most strongly resemble television screens receiving electronic static or "snow."

Like Götz, James Rosenquist also created a series of paintings during this period in which the pictorial surface evokes the surface of a television screen, even though his vision was very different. In 1966, Rosenquist produced a group of four paintings in the shape of television screens.[14] One painting from this series, *Aspen, Colorado*, at first glance resembles an abstract painting of the type that one might associate with the 1960s style of abstract painting, characterized by fields of color and occasionally painted on shaped canvases, that the critic Clement Greenberg termed "Post-Painterly Abstraction." It features a series of parallel stripes that seem to bow inward slightly, rendered in shifting hues of red, white, blue, black, and green that resonate with the arcs of the painting's left and right borders. The fact that the canvas is in the shape of a television screen, however, suggests that this work is not just an investigation of a purely formal problem. Indeed, the canvas's shape invites viewers to perceive the painting not as an exercise in pure abstraction but as a representation of a phenomenon familiar to all television viewers: interference. By suggesting a relationship between the pictorial surface and a television screen, Rosenquist thus good-naturedly seemed to poke fun at the pretensions of the Post-Painterly Abstractionists, who typically regarded their aesthetic enterprise as autonomous from the contamination of contemporary media culture.

As did Rosenquist, Robert Rauschenberg welcomed contemporary media culture's infiltration of the realm of painting. In his silkscreen paintings on canvas produced between 1962 and 1964, such as *Straw Boss* (1962), Rauschenberg printed the pictorial surface with photographic images linked by passages of gestural brushstrokes, drips, and spills. In these works there exists a spatially seamless flow of dematerialized images representing current events which are seemingly invested with the potential

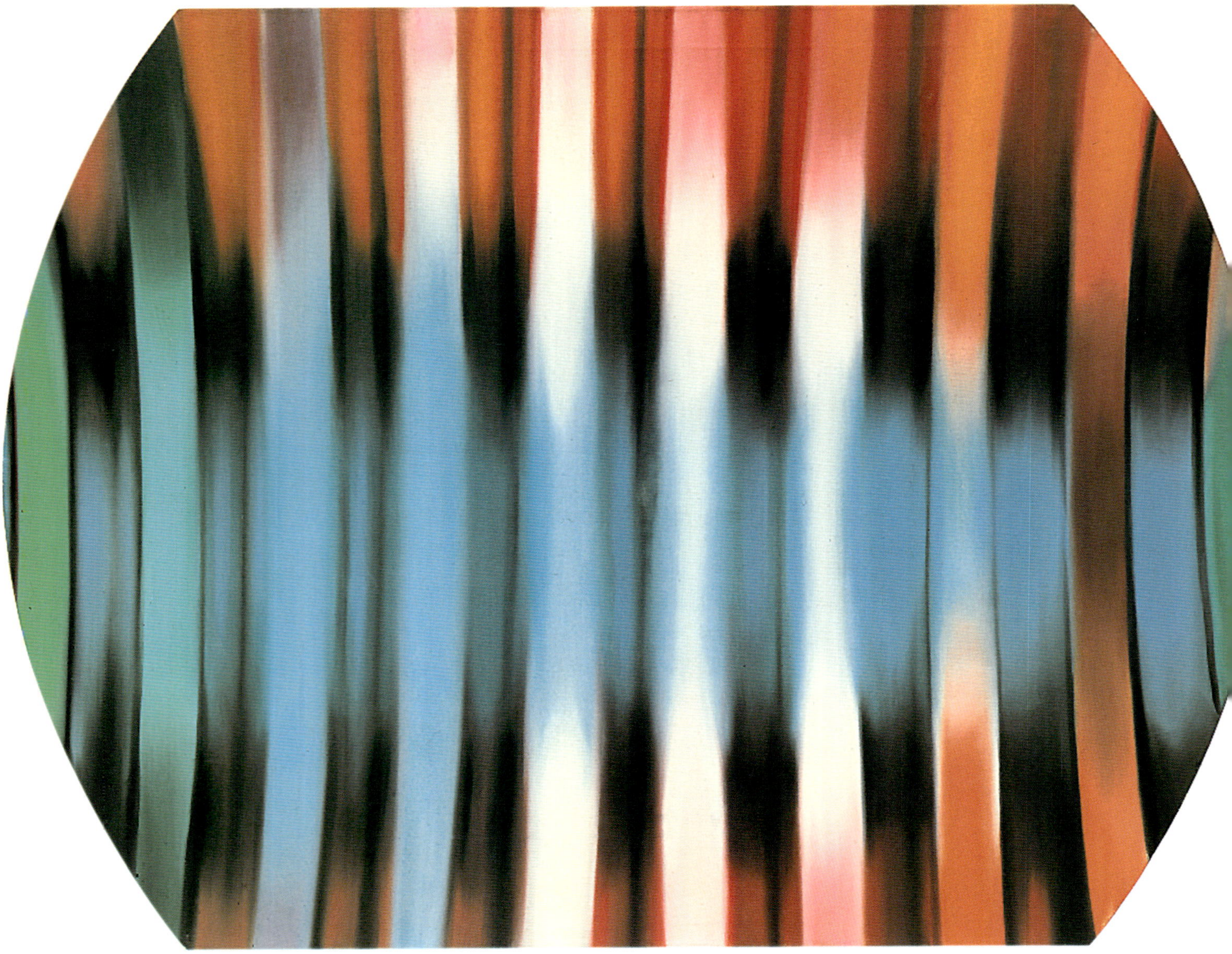

JAMES ROSENQUIST

Aspen, Colorado, 1966
Oil on canvas
48 × 62 inches (122 × 57 cm)
Private Collection
Courtesy Sonnabend Gallery, New York

for motion and are transformed in a manner evocative of the special effects employed in television programming. These compositions do not require the same kind of contemplative regard that certain premodernist and modernist paintings seem to require, where meaning is gleaned through sustained meditation. The diverse array of printed images in these works evokes the heterogeneous images broadcast on television news programs. The subjects of many of these images—orbiting satellites, running athletes, traffic-filled freeways—also suggest movement, a primary characteristic of the televisual image, as does their seeming liberation from the force of gravity, as they float buoyantly in a shallow space, interspersed with strokes, drips, wipes, and spills of paint. Moreover, unevenly printed, streaked with lines, and splattered with paint and turpentine, these images are just as distorted as the average televisual image of the period, when technological constraints and electrical interference typically resulted in such deformations as ghosting, portholing, mesh patterning, vertical and horizontal rolling, and moiré effect. Finally, the manipulation of these images by the artist evokes a variety of special effects that were used to edit the televisual image electronically at this time, including superimpositions, dissolves, wipes, inserts, and split screens.[15]

With his lithographic object *Shades* (1964), Rauschenberg took his silkscreen paintings one step closer to the televisual. This work consists of five Plexiglas panels on which he printed the same sort of images he used in the paintings on canvas. These panels, which may be inserted into an aluminum frame in any configuration, are illuminated from the back by a flashing light source. As the curator Dean Swanson observed in the catalogue for a 1964 exhibition, "*Shades* has both transparency and depth. The amalgam of familiar images is transitory—they are seen, then fade, only to reappear in new configurations with different priorities of perception."[16] In this manner, the substitution of plastic sheets for the canvas and the addition of a source of light that bathed viewers in its glow transformed the pictorial surface into a virtual television screen that lacked only the capacity for motion.

During the same period in which Rauschenberg was producing his silkscreen paintings, Wallace Berman was creating a series of mixed-media collages in which the pictorial surface manifests greater affinities with the televisual space of the screen than with the window or the mirror. One of the most ambitious of these works is *Papa's got a brand new bag* (1964), whose title is an homage to the song of the same name by the rhythm and blues pioneer James Brown, the "Godfather of Soul." In this work, photographic images torn from the pages of magazines and newspapers, along with other symbols, jostle against one another in a flow that

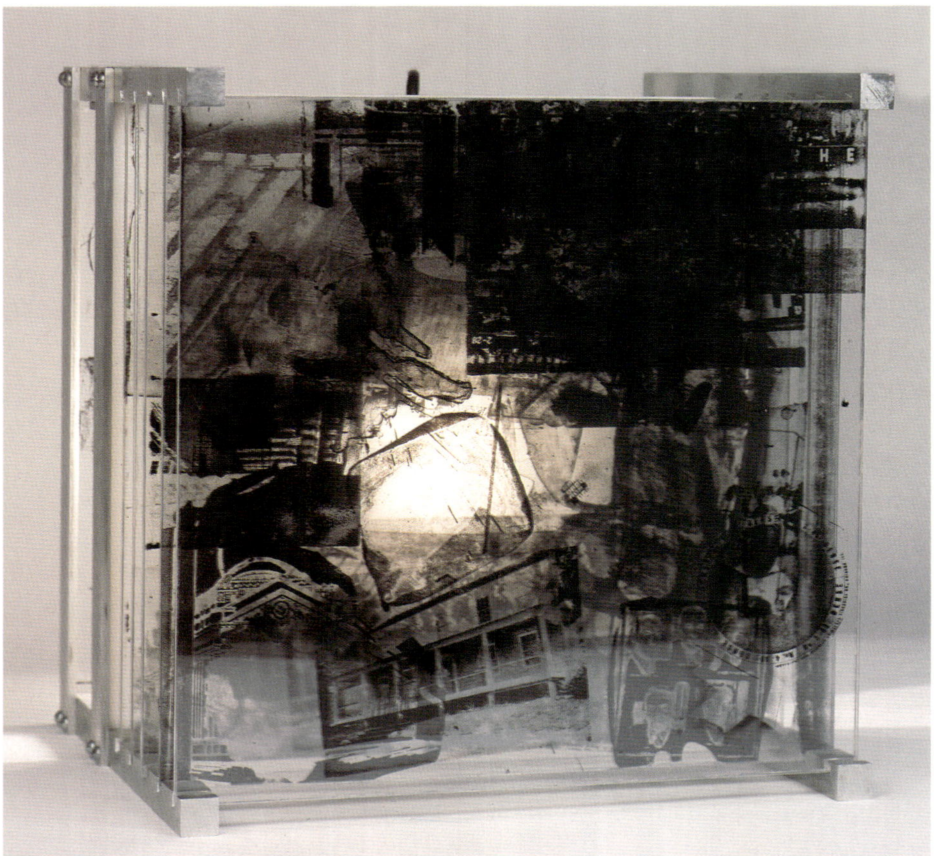

ROBERT RAUSCHENBERG

LEFT
Shades, 1964
Lithographic object consisting of six Plexiglas panels, aluminum frame, and light bulb
15 × 14 × 11¾ inches (38 × 36 × 30 cm)
Art Collection, Harry Ransom Humanities Research Center, The University of Texas at Austin

OPPOSITE
Straw Boss, 1962
Oil and silkscreen on canvas
96 × 60 inches (244 × 152 cm)
Weatherspoon Art Gallery, The University of North Carolina at Greensboro, Charles and Laura Dwan Memorial Gift, 1982

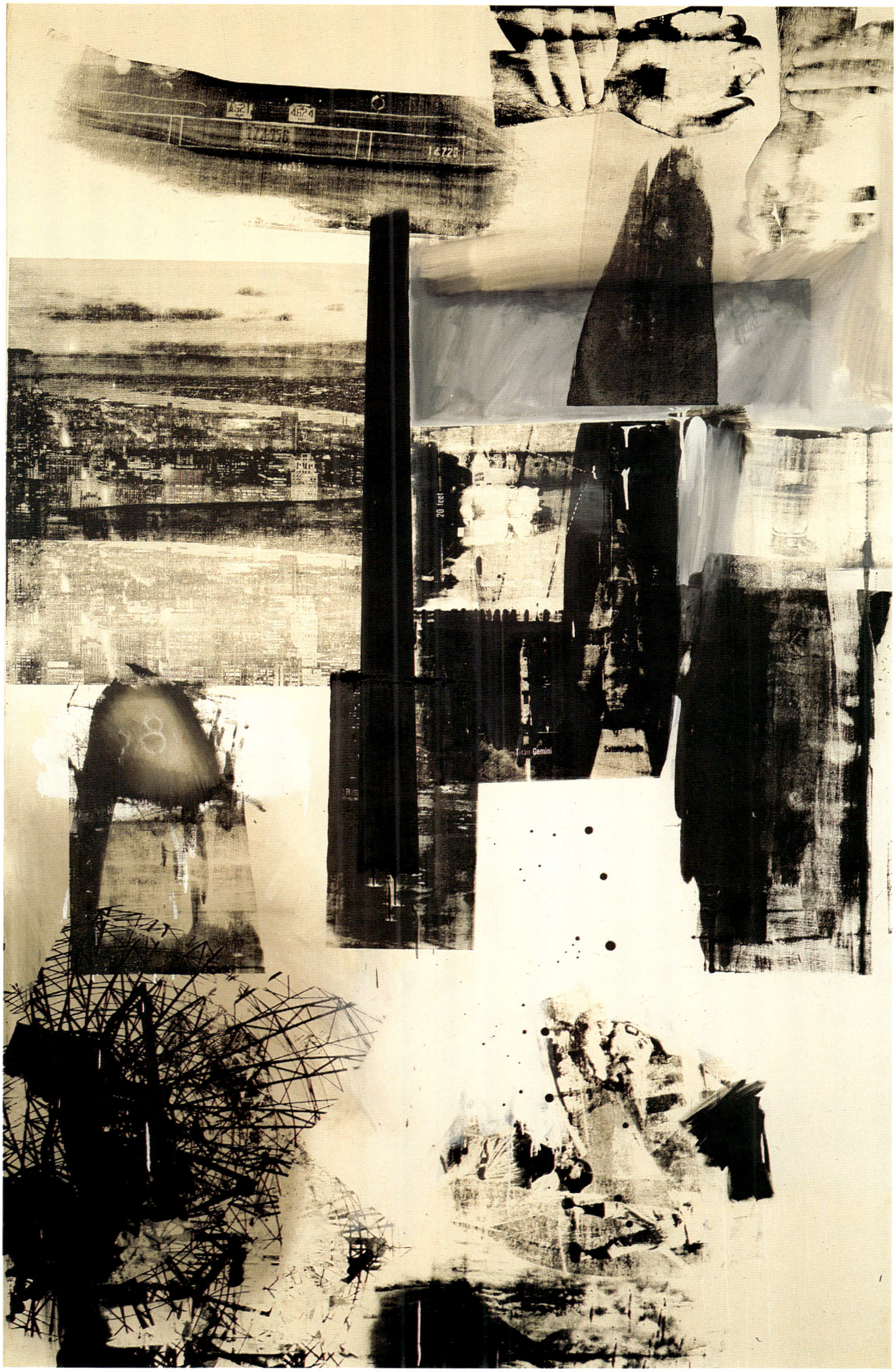
20 feet
Titan Gemini

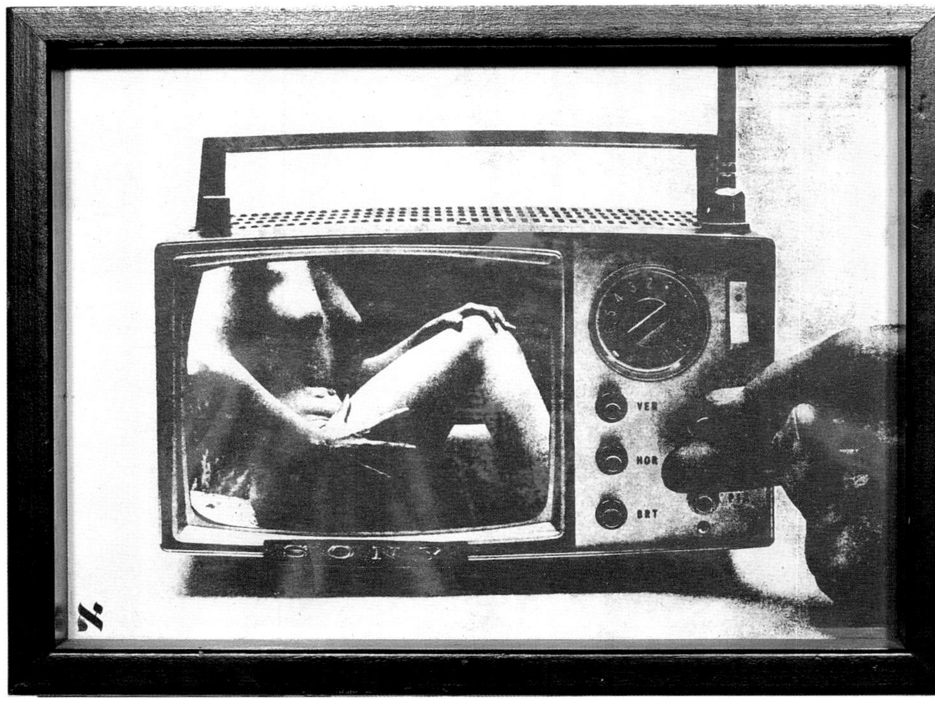

WALLACE BERMAN

Untitled, 1964
Verifax collage
$7\frac{1}{4} \times 9\frac{3}{4}$ inches (18×25 cm)
Collection of Dennis Hopper

animates the pictorial surface. To the left, for example, are depictions of Mick Jagger, Charlie Watts, and Keith Richards of the Rolling Stones; in the upper center are two repeated pictures of Cassius Clay (Muhammed Ali); and to the right is an image of Brown himself, affixed to the surface of a photograph of a hand-held transistor radio. Scattered throughout the pictorial field are Hebrew letters, such as aleph, mem, samekh, teth, waw, and he—ancient letters that do not form words with meaning, but seem to signify the elusiveness of meaning itself. The flatness of the surface evokes the flattened surface of the television screen. The repetition of images, only slightly different from one another, implies the mobile quality of the televisual image, represented literally in the center of the composition in the form of two portable television sets.

Like Berman, Ray Johnson created a series of collages that engaged with the mass media. *One TV* (1965) is one of his only works from this period that engages specifically with television. Diminutive in size, it consists of a sheet of paper on which he pasted a column of three postmarked Korean stamps, each one picturing a fisherman among a group of pelicans in the sea; to the right are the words "ONE TV," written in

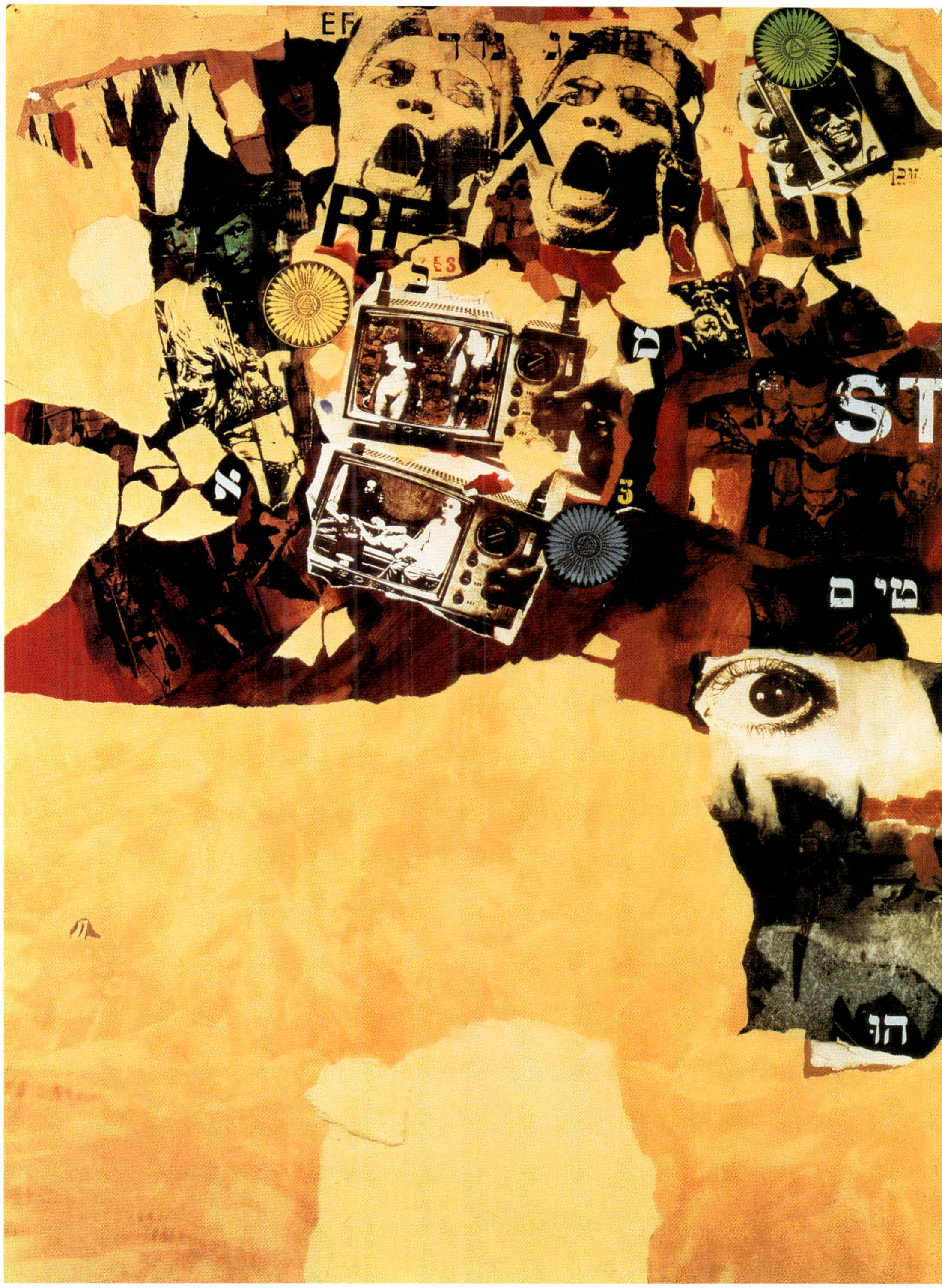

WALLACE BERMAN

Papa's got a brand new bag, 1964
Mixed media
42 × 30⅝ inches (107 × 78 cm)
Courtesy Nicole Klagsbrun Gallery, New York

block letters. In a manner typical of Johnson, the meaning of the relationship between the images and the words is elusive. But as the art historian Mason Klein has suggested, the imaging of water evokes the presence of a boundless system constantly in flux—a metaphor for television, in which an incessant flow of ever-changing images is transmitted across boundaries. "It is not by chance that Johnson invoked the specter of television in the title of this collage," Klein writes. "Within its imposed and secure boundaries, television automatically organizes its myriad discursive realities, allowing one to seamlessly interact with the outside world, without real contact, without ever feeling that something in one's environment has changed, without having to make sense of anything. And within this safe, continuous exchange of place, there is a kind of visual osmosis—an elimination of boundaries—as space and time merge, as objects and situations flow together, absorbed within a limitless totality."[17]

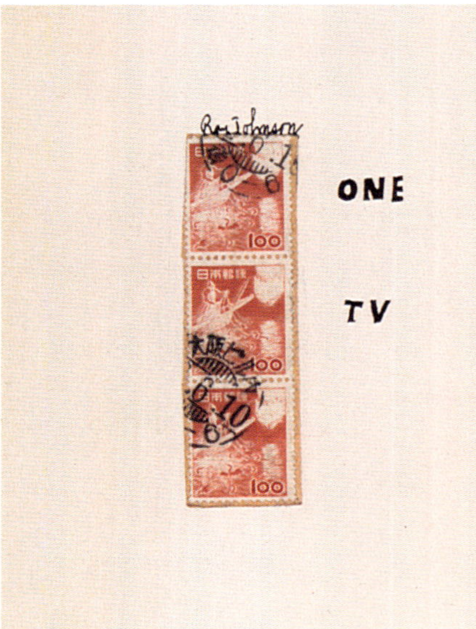

RAY JOHNSON

One TV, 1964
Ink and collage with Korean stamps
$5^{3}/_{8} \times 3^{7}/_{8}$ inches (14 × 10 cm)
Collection of William S. Wilson, New York

While Berman collaged images of television sets into the pictorial field and Johnson inscribed words, Tom Wesselmann incorporated actual working sets. In 1962, he produced two paintings, *Great American Nude #27* and *Great American Nude #39*, in which he collaged images of television sets into his work for the first time. A year later, he produced a pair of paintings, *Still Life #28* and *Still Life #31*, in which he replaced images of television sets with real ones. Each painting represents a domestic interior featuring an image of a table covered with a white and blue tablecloth. On each table is an image of a still-life arrangement consisting of a potted plant and a grouping of pears, as well as a real black-and-white television set, its screen flush with the pictorial surface, that seems to be resting on the table. In the background, hanging on the walls, are, respectively, portraits of Abraham Lincoln and George Washington. The flatness of the still lifes invokes the work of Paul Cézanne—the artist who, Marshall McLuhan claimed, abandoned the Renaissance-derived model of picture-making based on the ideal of perspectival illusionism, for a mode of representation that would eventually become disseminated through television. Moreover, the incorporation of collaged photographic images and of the television sets themselves addresses issues of flatness and illusion. If modernist artists such as Cézanne investigated this property in purely formal terms as the most essential property of painting, Wesselmann also engaged with it as a property exemplary of the visual dimension of the U.S. consumer culture of the 1960s. In Wesselmann's paintings, the flatness of the pictorial surface merges with that of the photographic image, which in turn merges with that of the television screen. All are

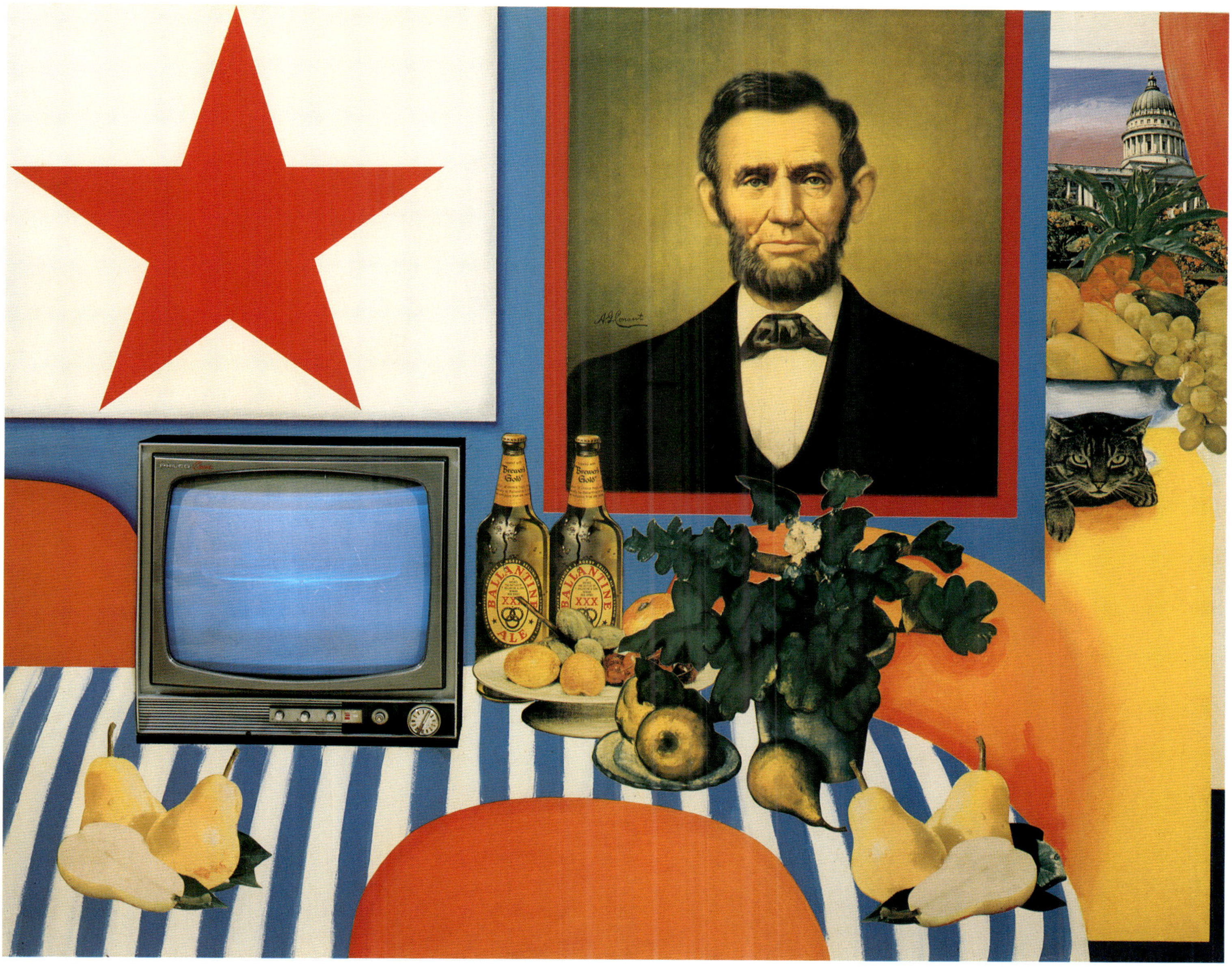

TOM WESSELMANN

Still Life #28, 1963
Acrylic, collage, and television set on board
48 × 60 inches (122 × 152 cm)
Collection of Robert E. Abrams

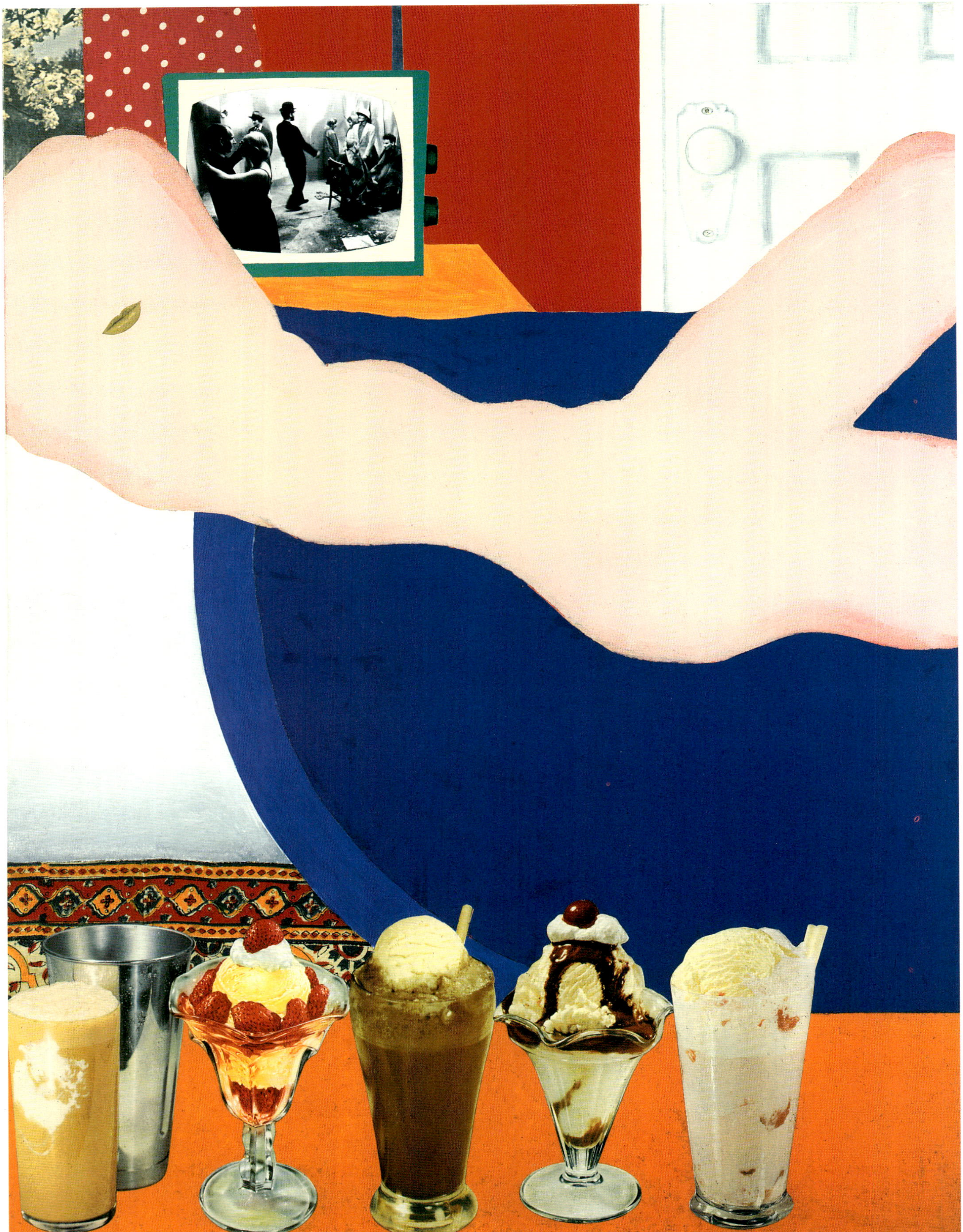

expressions of a culture in which the mass media were coming to assume an increasingly important role in the mediation of experience, a culture in which the accelerating proliferation of signs, models, and codes was becoming a primary constituent of social reality.

Circuits

In his *Exposition of Music Electronic Television*, presented at the Galerie Parnass in Wuppertal, West Germany, March 11–20, 1963, Nam June Paik premiered his "prepared television sets"—ordinary sets he had altered by modifying their electronic circuitry or by connecting them to other electronic devices. With these works, he contested the psychological and social implications of the naturalization of the state of passive distraction fostered through the experience of watching television. He sought to wrest viewers from their complacency, in some cases by making them distinctly uncomfortable. As he wrote in a text about the exhibition, "afterlude to the EXPOSITION of EXPERIMENTAL TELEVISION," published in the Fluxus newspaper *fLuxus cc fiVe ThReE* in June 1964:

> Anyway, if you see my TV, please, see it more than 30 minutes.
> "the perpetual evolution is the perpetual UNsatisfaction.
> It is the only merit of Hegelian dialectic."
> (R. AKUTAGAWA)
> "the perpetual Unsatisfaction is the perpetual evolution.
> It is the main merit of my experimental TV"
> (N.J.P.)
> The frustration remains as the frustration.
> There is NO catharsis.

In these sets, Paik altered the internal circuitry of actual television sets so that broadcast signals would be converted into distortions and abstractions. His initiation into the flourishing, interlinked avant-garde music and art scenes in West Germany in the late 1950s and early 1960s opened him up to a range of practices—Neo-Dada, Karlheinz Stockhausen's electronic music, K. O. Götz's electronic painting, and John Cage's cultivation of the indeterminate properties of electronic technology (which was derived in part from his study of Zen Buddhism). His intensive study of television electronics provided him with the requisite technical skills.

TOM WESSELMANN

Great American Nude #27, 1962
Enamel, casein, and collage
48 × 36 inches (122 × 91 cm)
The Mayor Gallery, London

NAM JUNE PAIK

Exhibition poster from
Exposition of Music Electronic Television
Galerie Parnass, Wuppertal,
Germany, March 1963
Silkscreen on newspaper and
offset on translucent paper with texts
by Nam June Paik and Jean-Pierre Wilhelm
Each sheet, 10 × 14 inches (25 × 36 cm)
Collection of Jon and Joanne Hendricks,
New York

Zen for TV, 1963/2000
Prepared television set
Dimensions variable
Collection of the Austin Museum of Art

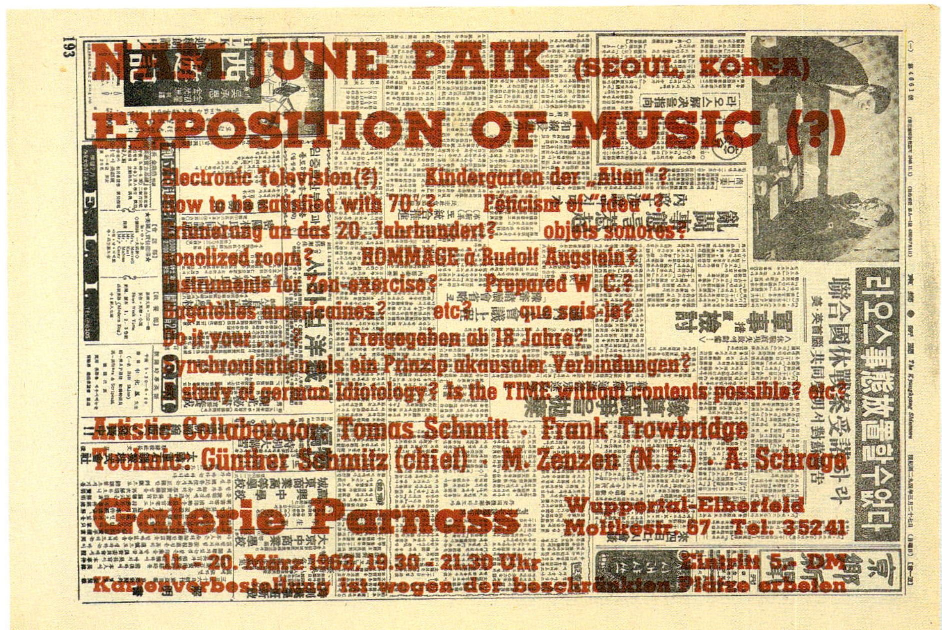

Although most of the works included in the *Exposition of Music Electronic Television* have been lost or destroyed, the exhibition can be reconstructed from textual accounts and photographs.[18] Visitors entered the gallery, housed in a villa, through a door from which the head of a freshly slaughtered ox was suspended. After passing through the foyer, they encountered what many contemporary reviewers described as the chaotic environment of a festival, in which numerous works, many of which engaged with the mass media, competed for their attention. In a room on the first floor were four "prepared pianos" (ordinary pianos that Paik had altered). On the second floor were *Prepared W.C.* (a bathroom filled with installations, including the head of a mannequin suspended over the toilet and the body of another mannequin lying in the bathtub); *To Be Naked and Look at Yourself* (pieces of tinfoil hung from the ceiling, allowing visitors to gaze at their distorted reflections); *Memory of the 20th Century* (magazines and newspapers strewn across the floor of a room); and other works. In the basement was a group of prepared record and tape players that visitors could play. And throughout the space were various "Instruments for Zen-Exercise"—musical instruments produced from ordinary objects that visitors could also manipulate.

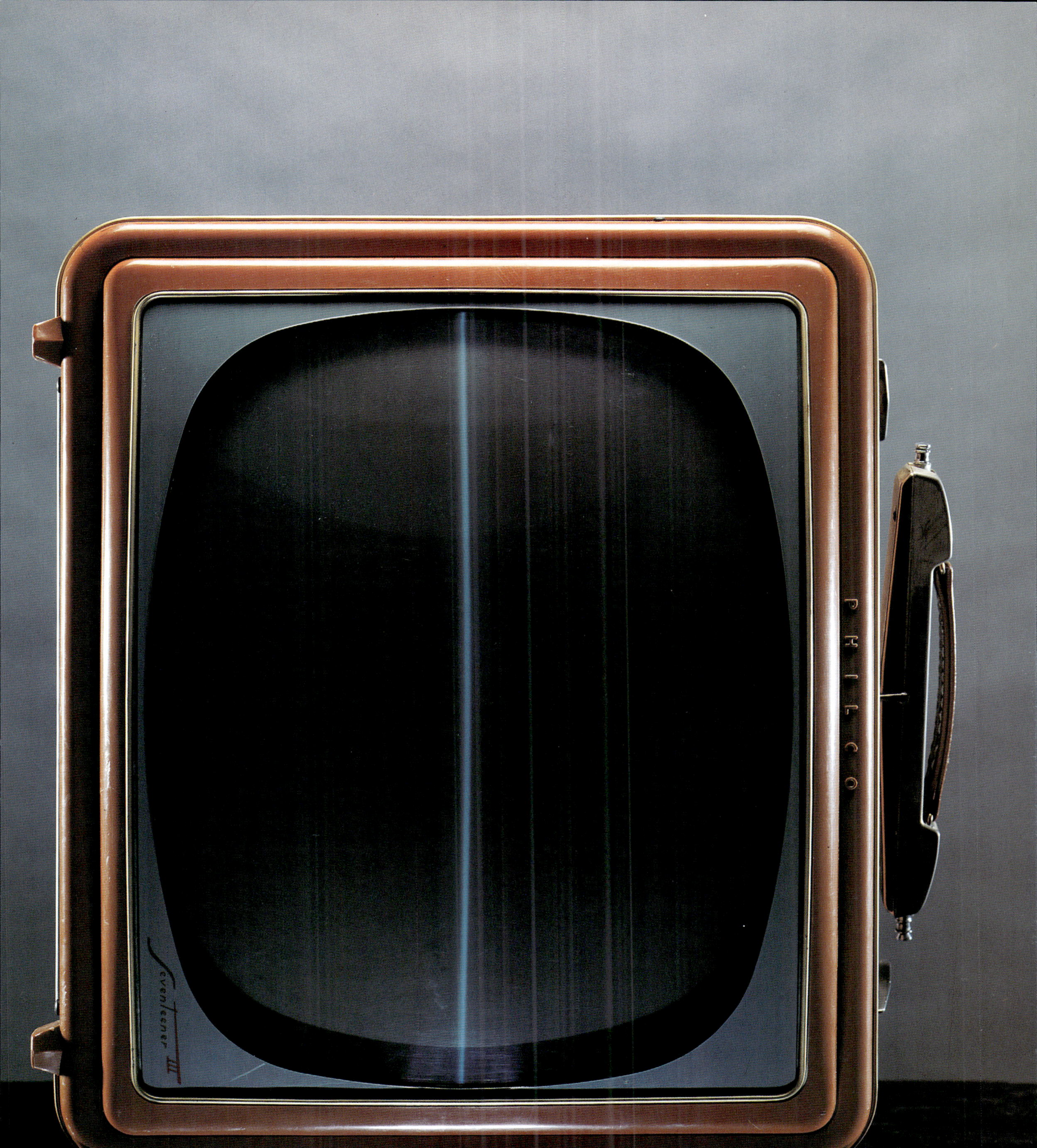
PHILCO
Seventeener III

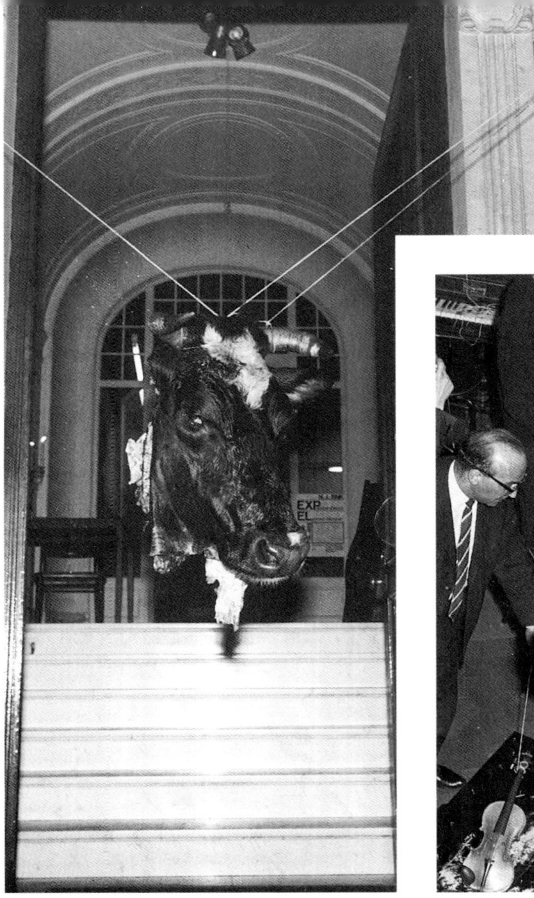

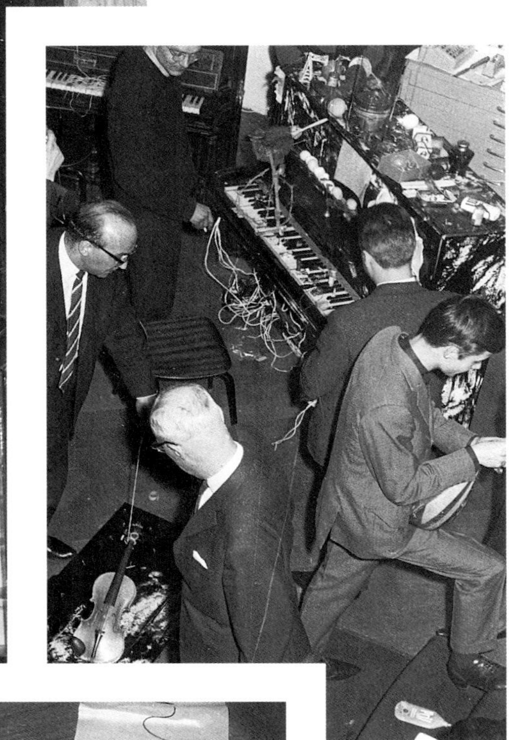

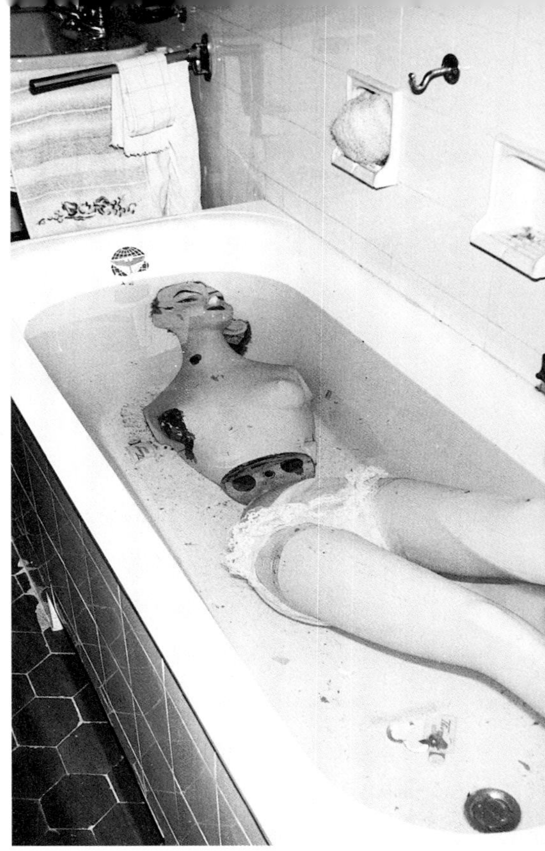

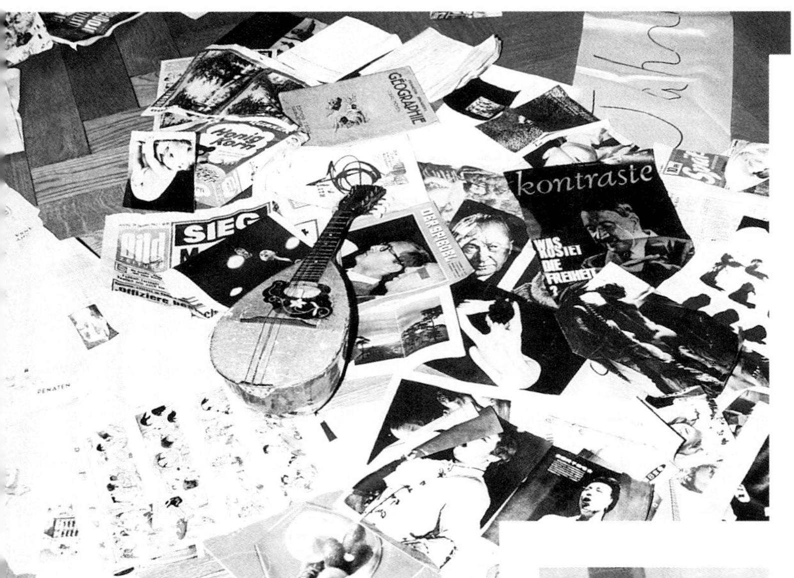
kontraste
SIEG

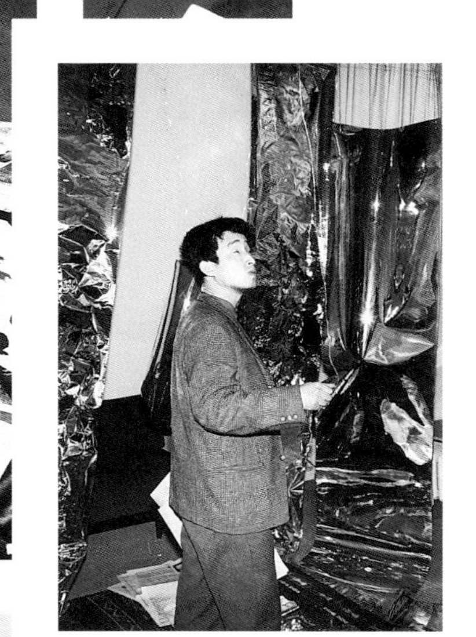

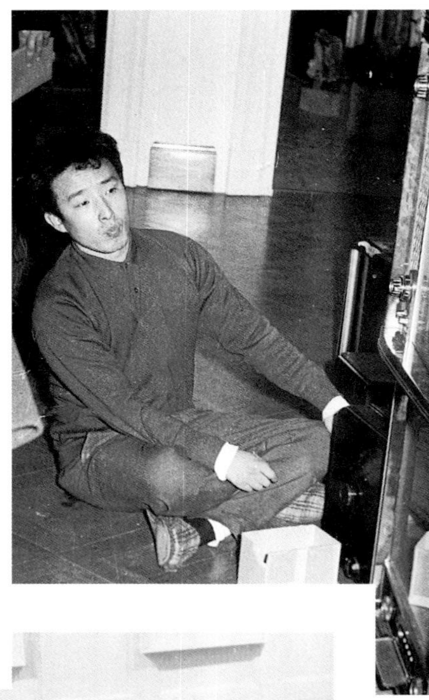

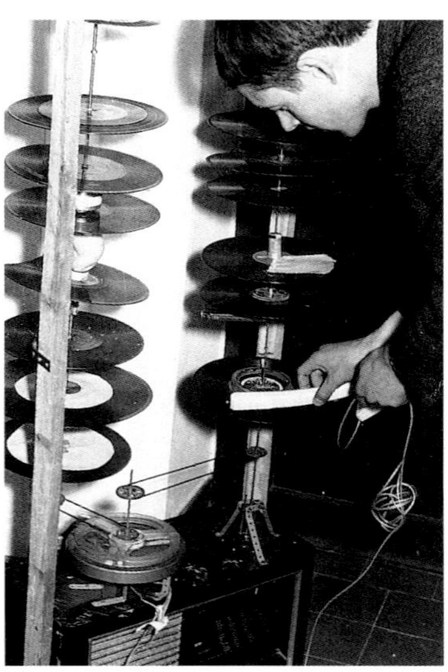

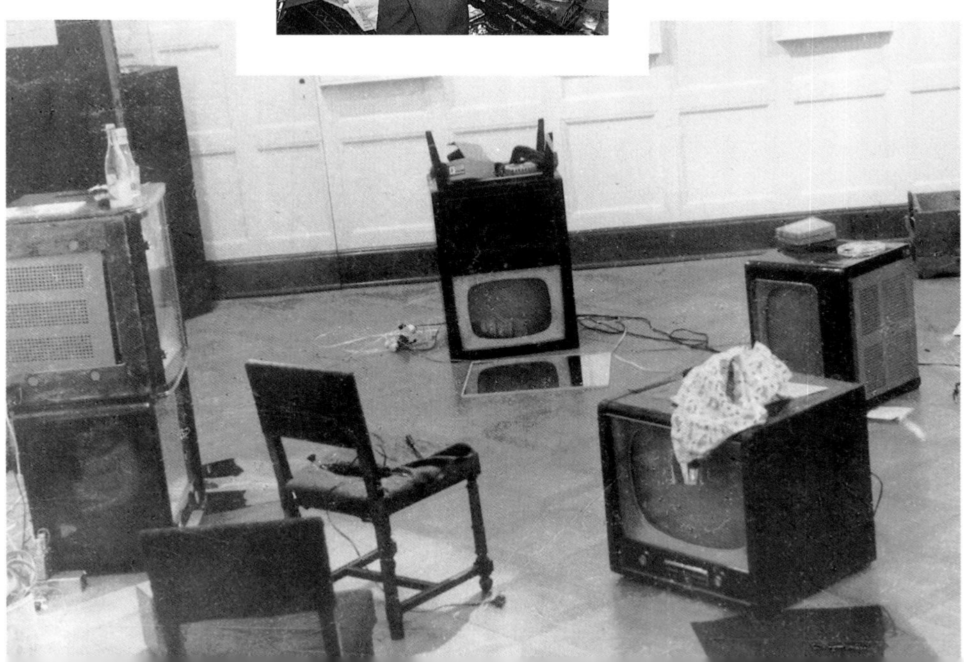

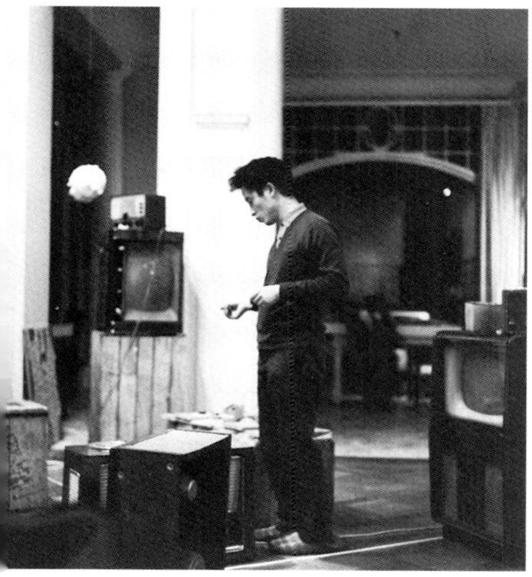

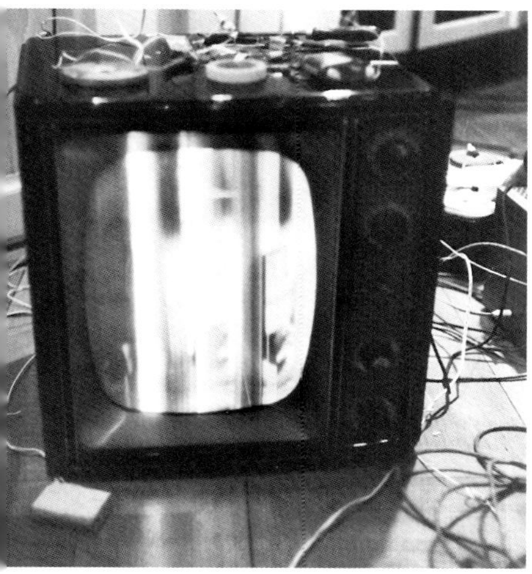

The highlight of the exhibition was a series of twelve or thirteen prepared television sets, all but one of which were installed in the sunroom on the first floor. Walking into the sunroom might have been like walking into a space colonized by a television set that had begun to reproduce and mutate uncontrollably. Except for a few chairs, there was little furniture; several sets, however, were arranged at random on the floor. In order to view or manipulate the sets, visitors were forced to bend over or squat down. While this encouraged visitors to perform repeated gestures of quasi-obeisance, it also introduced a physically active component into the process of viewing that contrasted with the conventional manner of watching television while seated or reclining.

Paik altered eight of the sets by modifying their electronic circuitry. These alterations produced the following effects: a vertical roll in negative; a picture rolled around a cylinder and modulated around the vertical axis; another picture rolled around a cylinder, but modulated around the horizontal axis; three independent sine waves; and a horizontal line. The last set served as the basis of another set, *Zen for TV*, which was altered in the same way but rotated ninety degrees so that its picture showed a vertical line. In addition, Paik altered four sets by connecting them to other electronic devices. These included a set connected to a floor switch, which, when stepped on, would cause points of light to splash across the screen and then vanish; a set connected to a microphone, which, when spoken into, would produce a similar effect; *Kuba TV* (a set connected to a tape recorder, so that the music played would determine the nature of the picture); and, situated on the floor, *One Point TV* (a set connected to a radio, the set's picture consisting of a point of light in the center of the screen that became larger as one increased the volume of the music).

In contrast to conventional sets, many of Paik's prepared sets were designed to be both watched and played. As such, they endowed visitors with a certain creative

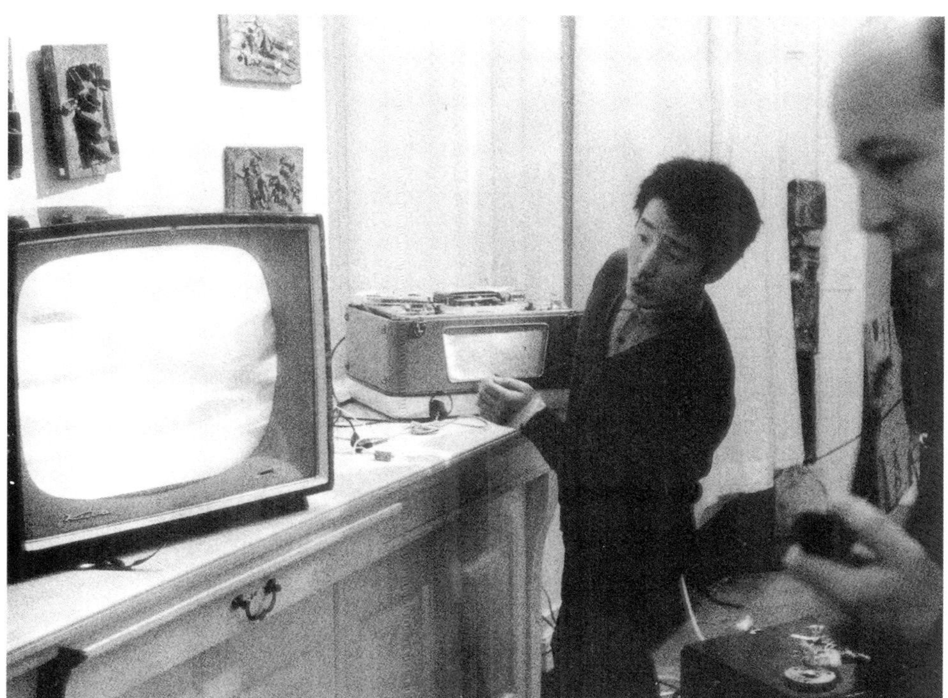

NAM JUNE PAIK

Documentation of *Exposition of Music Electronic Television*
Galerie Parnass, Wuppertal, Germany, March 1963:

OPPOSITE
Photographs by Rolf Jährling
Gelatin silver prints
8 × 10 inches (20 × 25 cm) or
10 × 8 inches (25 × 20 cm) each
The Gilbert and Lila Silverman Fluxus Collection, Detroit

ABOVE
Photographs by George Maciunas
Gelatin silver prints
10 × 8 inches (25 × 20 cm) each
The Gilbert and Lila Silverman Fluxus Collection, Detroit

RIGHT
Photograph by Manfred Leve
Gelatin silver print
9½ × 11⅞ inches (24 × 30 cm)
Courtesy Galerie Berndt Kunsthandel GmbH, Cologne

PETER MOORE

"Double-yoke experiments" from *Distorted TVs*, from the exhibition *Electronic Art*, Galería Bonino, New York, November 1965
Gelatin silver print
8 × 10 inches (20 × 25 cm)
Courtesy Estate of Peter Moore/ Bound & Unbound, New York

Nam June Paik with original *Demagnetizer* (or *Life Ring*)
New York, October 1965
Gelatin silver print
8 × 10 inches (20 × 25 cm)
Courtesy Estate of Peter Moore/ Bound & Unbound, New York

Nam June Paik with *Magnet TV*, New York, October 1965
Gelatin silver print
8 × 10 inches (20 × 25 cm)
Courtesy Estate of Peter Moore/ Bound & Unbound, New York

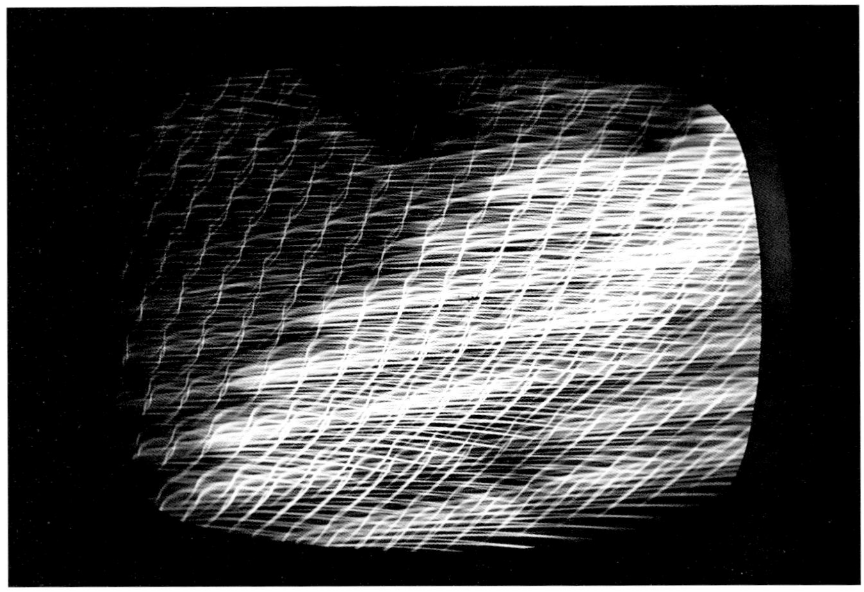

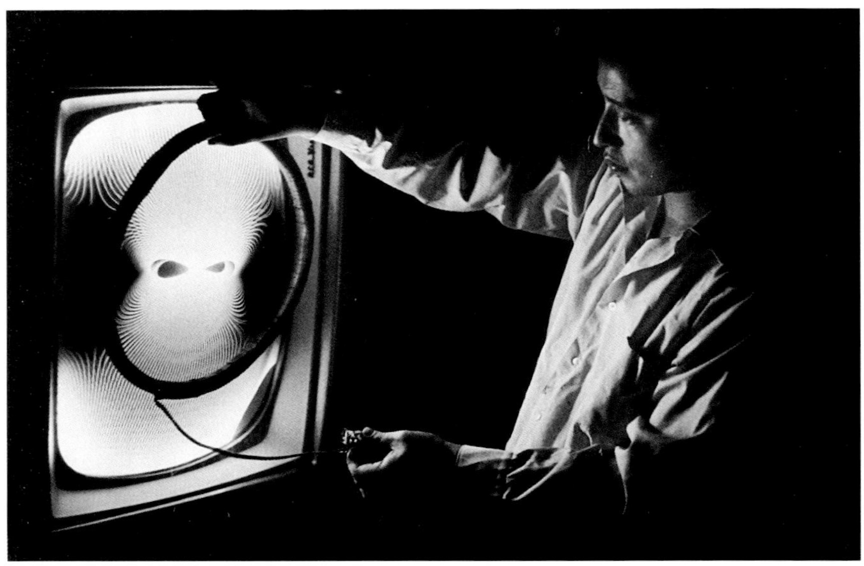

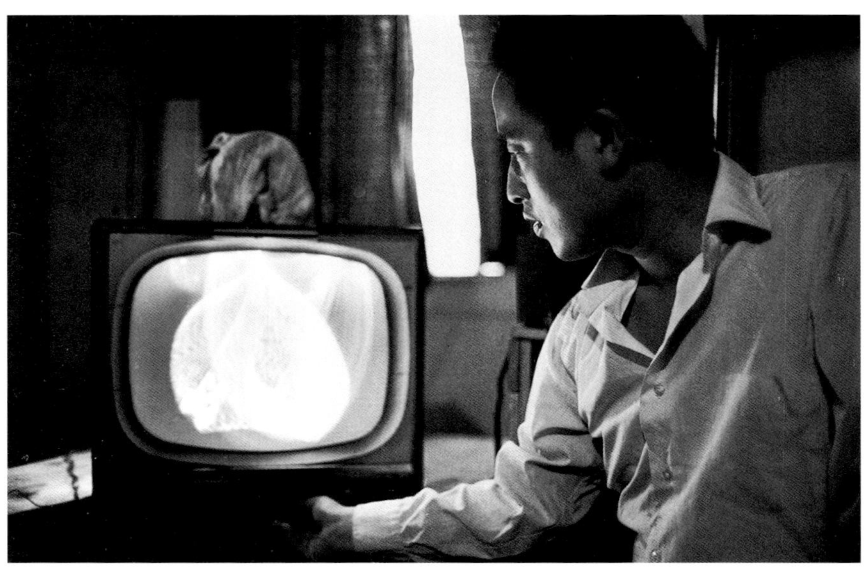

freedom by encouraging them to perceive the television set not simply as a piece of furniture, but as a sculpture that demanded their active physical, psychological, and perceptual involvement. He maintained that this attentive and engaged mode of viewing had the potential to induce a radical transformation of consciousness in viewers, a change he conceived as a type of Zen enlightenment, as they began to understand that desire, a drive that is exploited by advertisers to encourage ever-increasing rates of consumption, is the root of unhappiness.

In her work *Sky TV* (1966), Yoko Ono also sought to extricate viewers from the circuits of power in which they had become integrated by disrupting the flow of standard broadcast transmissions. This work, which Ono described as a "furniture piece," exists as the following instruction: "A closed circuit TV set up in the gallery for looking at the sky." The work may be exhibited as this instruction and realized only in the imaginations of visitors, or it may be executed. When it is executed, a videocamera is installed on the exterior of the exhibition building and pointed toward the sky. The images the camera records are transmitted in real time to a television set installed in the exhibition space. Depending on what is in the camera's field of vision, viewers consequently see fields of blue, gray, or other colors, interspersed with birds, airplanes, or other creatures or objects that pass randomly by the camera's eye, rather than programs and commercials. Because these images are independent of conventional broadcast programming, they do not address viewers as the products that the networks promise to deliver to their advertisers. Instead, they liberate them from this circuit by showing the poetic and the political possibilities of an alternative television that is not beholden to the imperatives of capitalist modernity.

Like Paik and Ono, Wolf Vostell also sought to develop strategies that liberated viewers from the state of passive distraction promoted by television. He derived these strategies from his concept of *dé-coll/age*, which he defined as an aesthetic and social practice through which an act of destruction is transformed into an act of creation. Vostell accepted the reality of destruction in contemporary society, but at the same time he sought to transform it into a constructive force that would facilitate the development in viewers of emancipatory modes of perception, cognition, and behavior. The focus of his efforts was the psychological violence perpetrated by the mass media. Consequently, in the 1950s he began to produce a series of *dé-coll/ages*, often as public performances that involved the participation of the audience. He would tear through layers of posters pasted on top of one another, smear the pages of mass-circulation magazines with tissues soaked in solvent,

WOLF VOSTELL

BELOW
TV für Millionen (TV for Millions), 1959/65
Tuned television set
$19^{3}/_{4} \times 22^{1}/_{2} \times 17^{3}/_{4}$ inches ($50 \times 57 \times 45$ cm)
Museum of Modern Art Ludwig Foundation
Vienna, formerly Hahn Collection, Cologne

OPPOSITE
Page spread from
TV-dé-coll/age: & Morning Glory: 2 pieces, 1963
Artist's book (New York: Smolin Gallery, 1963)
$6 \times 4 \times 2$ inches ($15 \times 10 \times 5$ cm)
Rare Books and Manuscripts, The Ohio
State University Libraries, Columbus

and distort television broadcasts, transforming the messages they transmitted to the point of near-illegibility. By strategically destroying posters, magazine pages, and television broadcasts, he uncovered in an almost archaeological manner the layers of psychological and social authority encoded within them: the conditions that sustained the subjection of consumers to the rule of the commodity.

In the late 1950s, Vostell began to *dé-coll/age* television broadcasts in works such as *TV für Millionen* (TV for Millions, 1959–66). Inspired by images of malfunctioning television sets he saw in a 1959 book on television repair, he was led to vandalize the medium of television, as he had vandalized posters and magazine pages. In contrast to the prepared television sets that Paik would develop in the early 1960s, Vostell distorted broadcast transmissions not by altering the sets' electronic circuitry, but by manipulating their controls—the antenna, dial, brightness knob, vertical and horizontal hold knobs, and so on. The stable contours of the images of bodies visible on the screens of properly functioning television sets were grotesquely stretched out of shape in continuous deformation; parallel lines or waves that slashed across the screen represented the strategically induced failure of broadcast signals to be perceived as intended by the networks.

Vostell conceived his project *TV-dé-coll/age-Ereignisse für Millionen* (TV-dé-coll/age-Events for Millions, 1959/63) as a program to be broadcast on a television network to millions of viewers. Although such a broadcast never occurred, he did perform excerpts from the performance score on May 19, 1963, on the artist George Segal's farm near South Brunswick, New Jersey, as part of the Yam Festival, a series of events organized by the Fluxus artists George Brecht and Robert Watts that took place throughout the month ("Yam" is "May" spelled backward). As he writes in the preface to the score, *TV-dé-coll/age-Ereignisse für Millionen* was "planned as a television

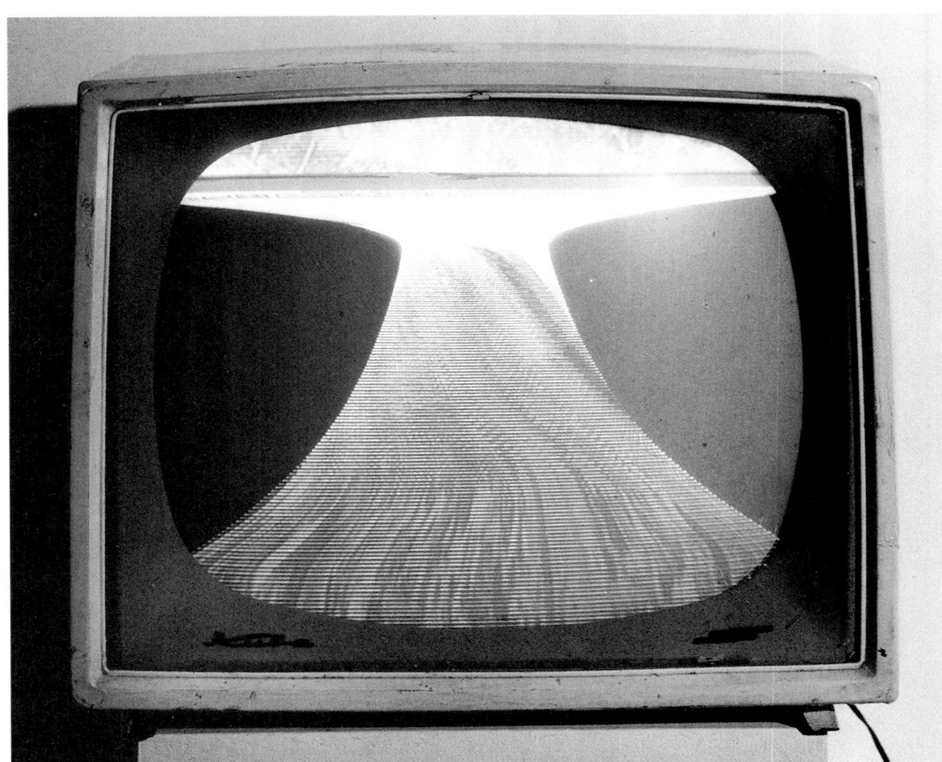

program in which the televiewers take part/to be performed alone in front of the TV screen in a closed room."[19] The score, consisting of a list of actions to be performed, was published in the book *dé-coll/age happenings* in 1966, and also exists graphically in the form of two drawings. Vostell also produced an artist's book entitled *TV-dé-coll/age: & Morning Glory; 2 pieces*, published by the Smolin Gallery in New York in 1963, with another version of the score; this version was the basis for his Yam Festival performance.

Had the program been broadcast as intended, it would have been unlike any program ever seen on television. It began with three minutes of static, followed by an anonymous announcer instructing viewers to perform a series of seemingly absurd actions, as this excerpt suggests:

> hide your face
> sit directly in front of the screen and brush your teeth
> look at the faces and think as you see each one
> *where was this face 17 years ago?*
> hold your naked stomach in front of the screen and drink a coca-cola while thinking about
> pepsi cola ads
> walk or crawl around the room and repeat everything said on the program
> lie down under the bedcovers with a micro tv set
> turn on all the household appliances and wrap up your tv set with barbed wire
> feed the television set a tv dinner.

By performing such activities, viewers could achieve a heightened awareness of the extent to which they had unconsciously invested television with a human dimension: a soul.

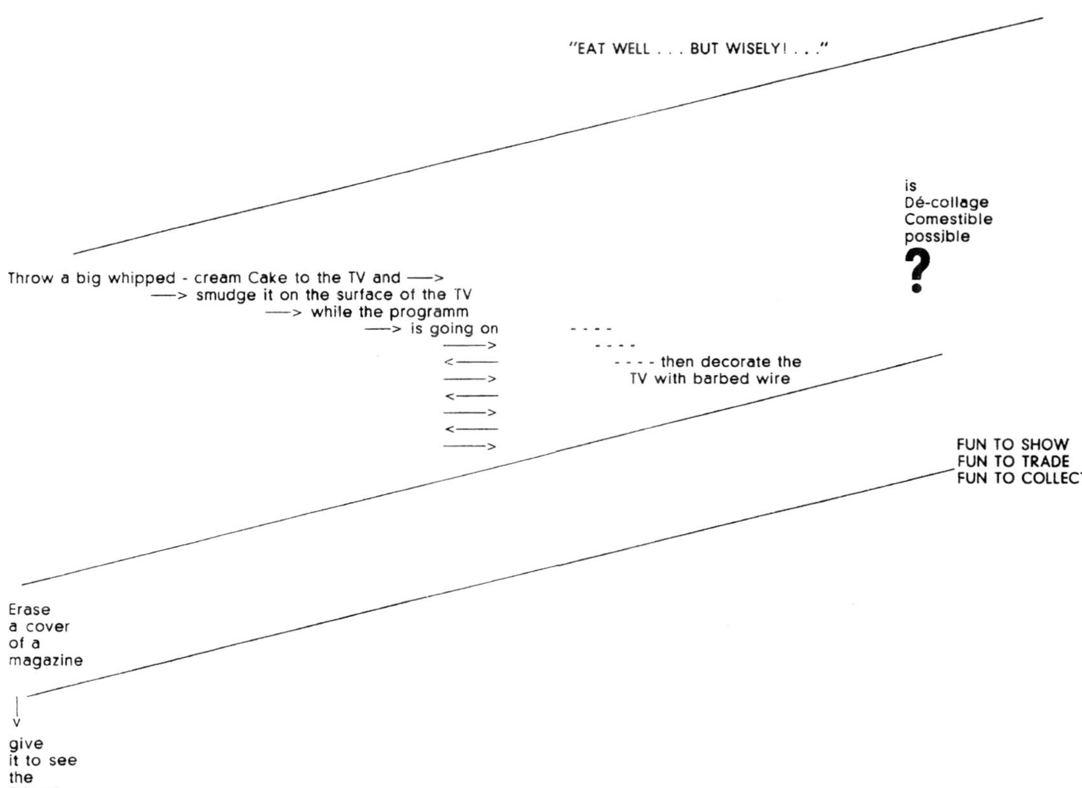

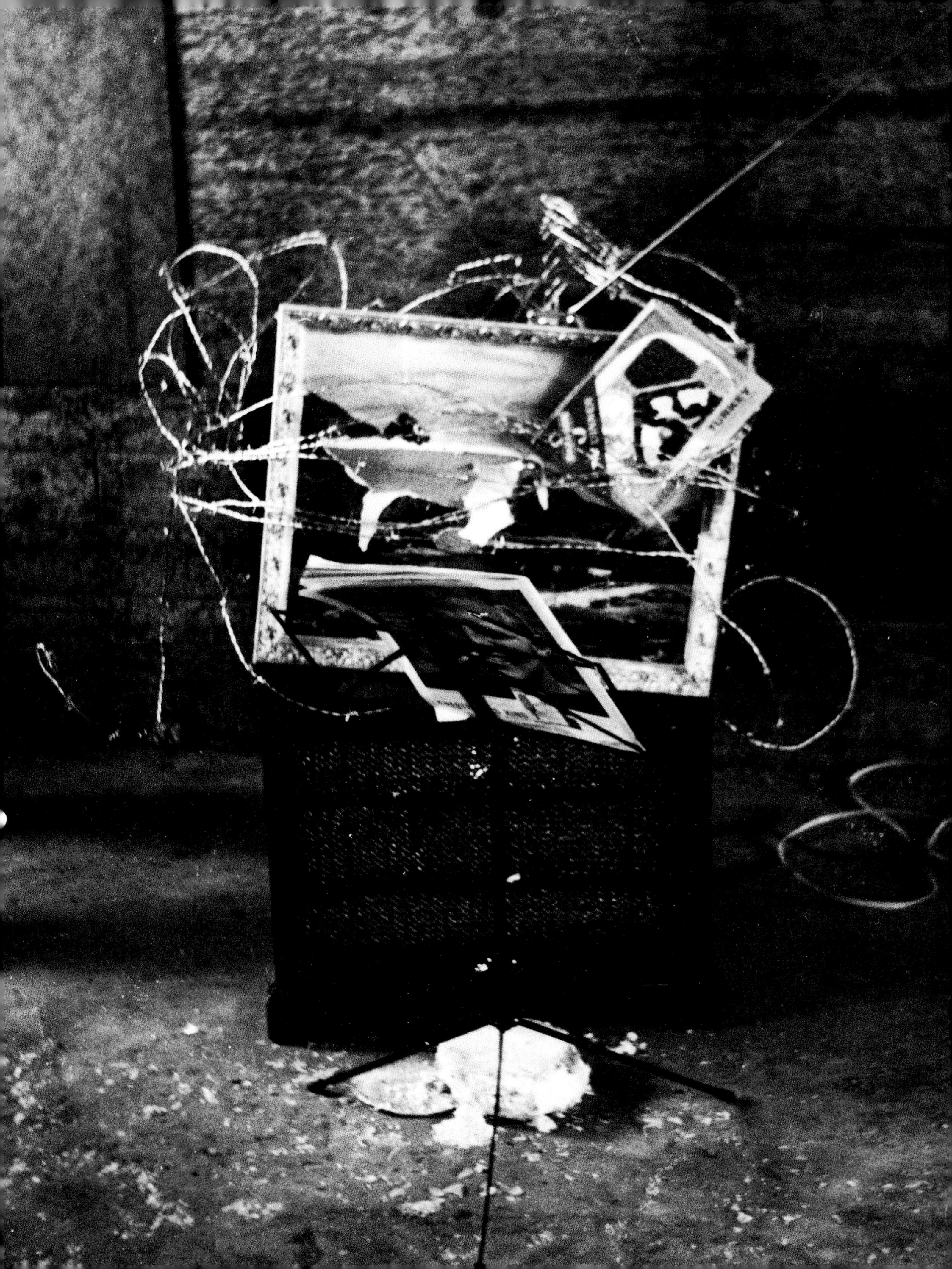
TURKEY

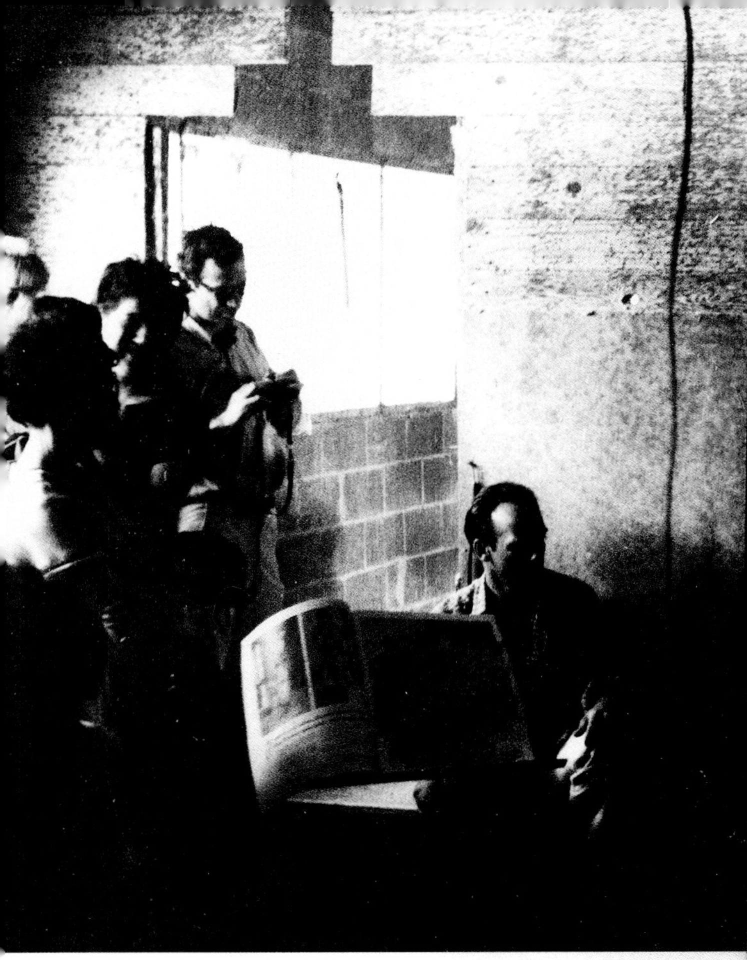
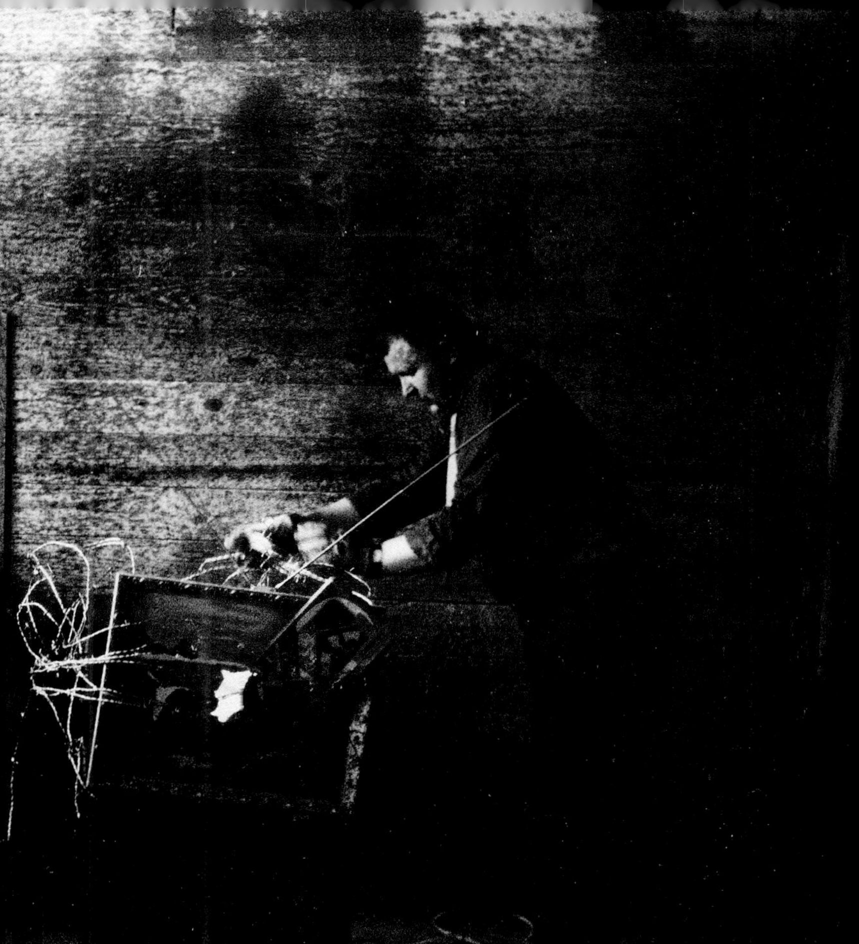
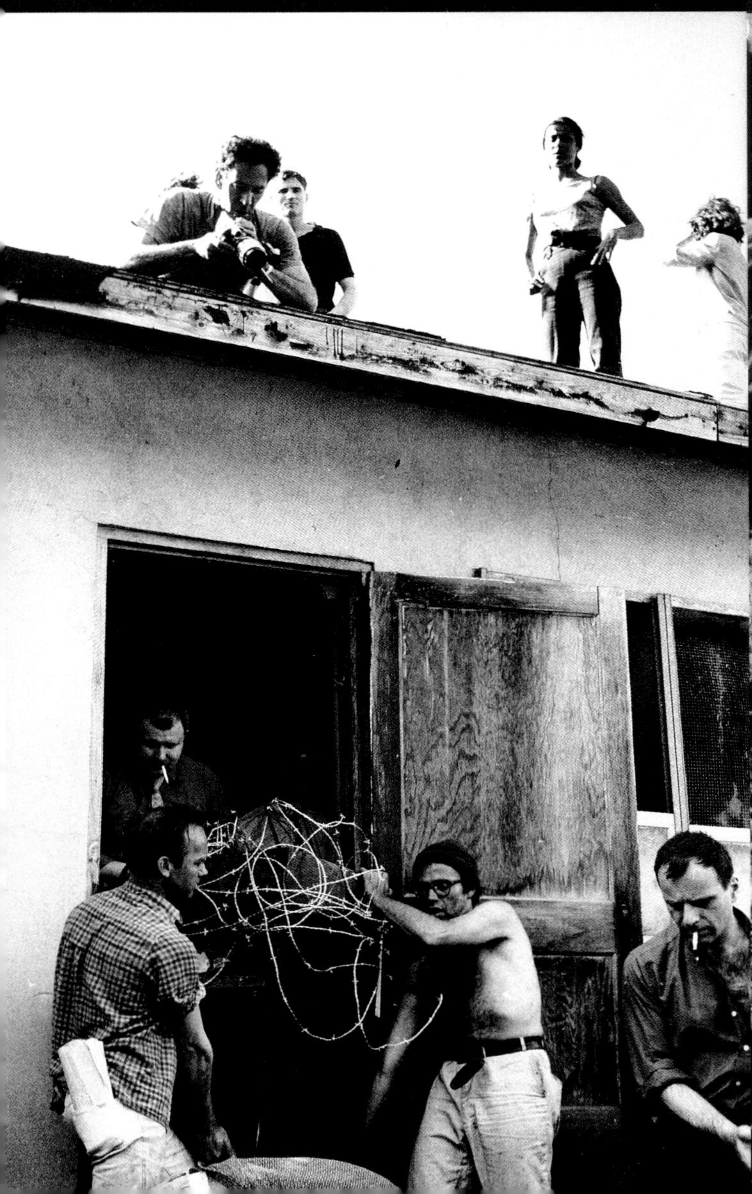
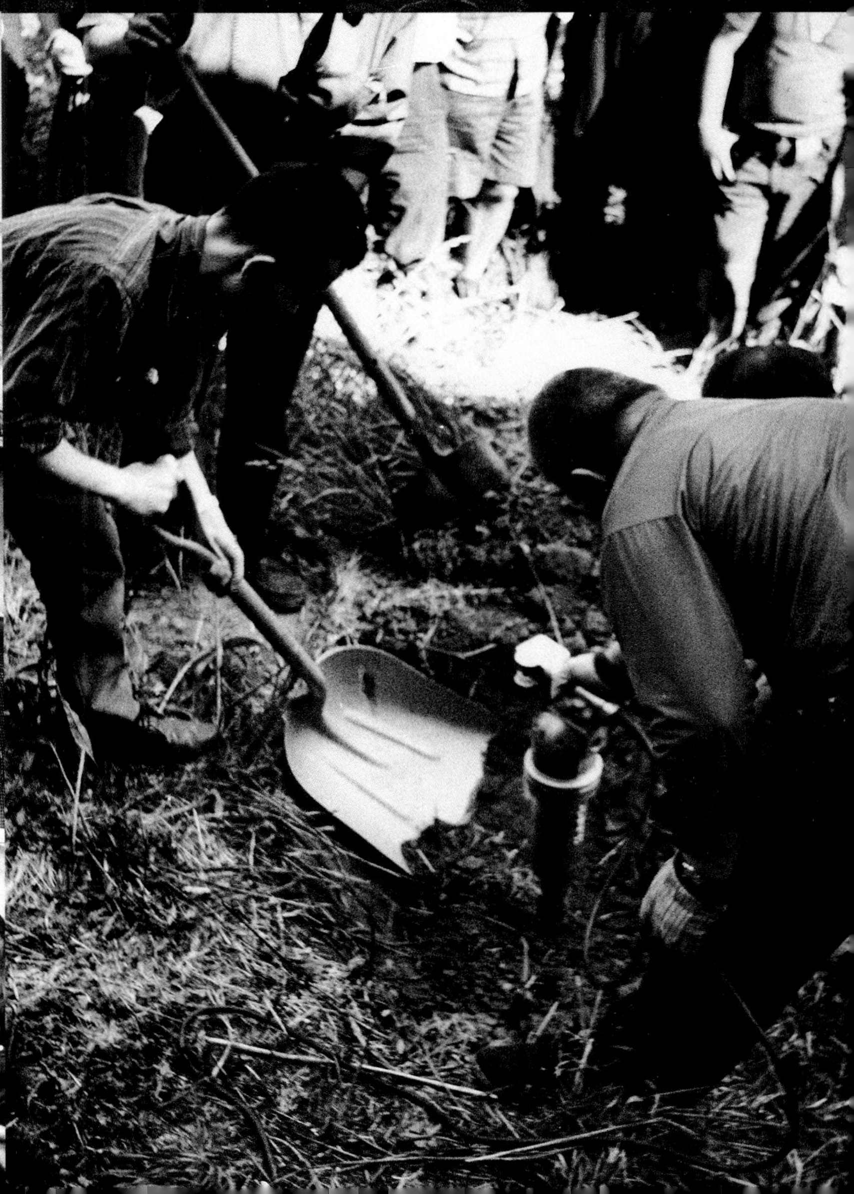

PRECEDING PAGES
Documentation of performance of *TV-dé-coll/age* action performed on George Segal's farm near South Brunswick, New Jersey, May 19, 1963
Photographs by Peter Moore
Gelatin silver prints
8 × 10 inches (20 × 25 cm) or 10 × 8 inches (25 × 20 cm) each
Courtesy Estate of Peter Moore/Bound & Unbound, New York

The investment of commodities with a psychic dimension was one of the strategies used by an influential mode of advertising that emerged in the post–World War II period and was based on the science of motivation research. Before World War II, advertisers had largely relied on marketing research—the collection and analysis of empirical data about consumers' conscious purchasing preferences—to determine how best to maximize consumption of their products. After the war, through techniques derived from psychoanalysis, psychology, anthropology, and sociology, motivation researchers attempted to uncover the subconscious and unconscious motivations that influenced consumers' decisions to buy certain products—impulses that would explain why consumers preferred one brand over another when both were essentially the same. For example, as Dr. Ernst Dichter, the pioneer of motivation research, wrote in *The Strategy of Desire* (1960), "If I can describe a cake, a cigarette, a fishing rod, or a bottle of whiskey in such a way that its basic soul, its basic meaning to the modern man, becomes clear, I shall have at the same time achieved direct communication, I shall have established a bridge between my ad and the reader and come as close as possible to motivating the reader or listener to acquire this experience via the product which I have promised him."[20]

The development of marketing strategies that exploited the unconscious motivations that determined consumers' desires for certain products was the subject of Vance Packard's 1957 bestseller, *The Hidden Persuaders*, which characterized Dichter as an ominous figure. Dichter's institute, Packard wrote, is a "mansion where you are apt to see children watching TV sets. The TV room has concealed screens behind which unseen observers sometimes crouch, and tape recorders are planted to pick up the children's happy or scornful comments. Dr. Dichter has a 'psycho-panel' of several hundred families in the area whose members have been carefully charted as to their emotional make-up. The institute knows precisely how secure, ambitious, realistic, and neurotic each member is (if he is); and thus by trying out various subtle advertising appeals on these indexed people the institute can purportedly tell what the response might be to a product geared, say, to the hypochondriac or social climber."[21]

In *TV-dé-coll/age-Ereignisse für Millionen*, Vostell offered an alternative spectatorship that forced viewers to become aware of the extent to which the practice of watching television resulted in the conscious and unconscious internalization of cognitive and behavioral patterns. These patterns produced obedience to the strategies of desire that advertisers used to promote the consumption of commodities. As previously stated, he was never able to broadcast *TV-dé-coll/age-Ereignisse für Millionen* as he had intended; however, he performed excerpts from the score at the Yam Festival. As a series of photographs by Peter Moore reveals, the performance began in a shed, where a handful of spectators witnessed Vostell subject a television set to a series of defilements from the last half of the score, as presented in *TV-dé-coll/age: & Morning Glory; 2 pieces*. In addition to throwing a cake at the set, he ripped the canvas of a framed painting, placed it over the screen, and wrapped the set with barbed wire, into which he stuck a Swanson's TV dinner (turkey). He also used solvents to smear the pages of a magazine, which he placed on a music stand in front of the set. With the assistance of several others, Vostell then carried the set to a field, where he dug a hole in the ground with a jackhammer and a shovel and buried the set. By subjecting the set to a series of progressively destructive actions that interfered with the smooth transmissions of the televisual flow, Vostell disrupted the ability of programming to position viewers as consumers through the conscious and unconscious inculcation of the imperative to buy. Moreover, by using commodities like the cake, the TV dinner, and even the painting to defile the television set, the instrument through which the imperative to consume was transmitted, he turned the act of consumption against itself.

Spectacles

At 1:40 p.m., Eastern Standard Time, on Friday, November 22, 1963, CBS News interrupted the network's broadcast of *As the World Turns*. The disembodied voice of Walter Cronkite announced: "In Dallas, Texas, three shots were fired at President Kennedy's motorcade in downtown Dallas. The first reports say that President Kennedy has been seriously wounded by this shooting. . . . Stay tuned to CBS News for further details." Afterward, *As the World Turns* resumed as usual until the second commercial break, when regular programming was suspended for the duration of a crisis that the mass media would package as the "Four Dark Days," spanning the time from the assassination to the burial of the president. Television's coverage of the Kennedy assassination and its aftermath accelerated a process whose effects are now clearly apparent: the investment of the medium with the authority not only to mediate the experience of reality but also to produce it. Television, commentators asserted, allowed viewers to experience the assassination and the events that followed as if they were eyewitnesses; it electronically united the nation in a community of grief; and it refrained from exploiting the tragedy of President Kennedy's death. In their descriptions of the experience of television spectatorship during the crisis, commentator after commentator suggested that television's status as a visual medium gave viewers direct access to actual events in real time by circumventing the mediation of language, as well as by transmitting visual images in real time. These properties in turn accelerated the process by which the relationship of viewers to the electronic images they witnessed on the screen was dramatically reforged. Electronic images were invested with an almost material presence, while the material world was enveloped into the realm of the electronic image. As one commentator remarked in *TV Guide*, "Thus what happened on the television screen became in every sense an epic drama four days long, in which the viewers were not so much spectators as participants."[22] In this passage, the historical events of the Four Dark Days are defined as a veritable television program in which the actors are not only President and Mrs. Kennedy, Lee Harvey Oswald, and Walter Cronkite, et al., but also the viewers themselves—testimony to the medium's colonization of the physical world. While commentators generally stopped short of questioning the cultural implications of this phenomenon, artists such as Dennis Hopper, Andy Warhol, and Bruce Conner found this rich territory to explore.

In *Kennedy Funeral* (1963), his series of black-and-white photographs of broadcasts of the aftermath of the assassination, Dennis Hopper demythologized the networks' coverage of the crisis by emphasizing the status of the electronic images as mediated representations. Hopper shot the photographs by pointing his camera directly at a television screen. The edges of the screen extend to the borders of each photograph, each of which arrests an image from the televisual flow that

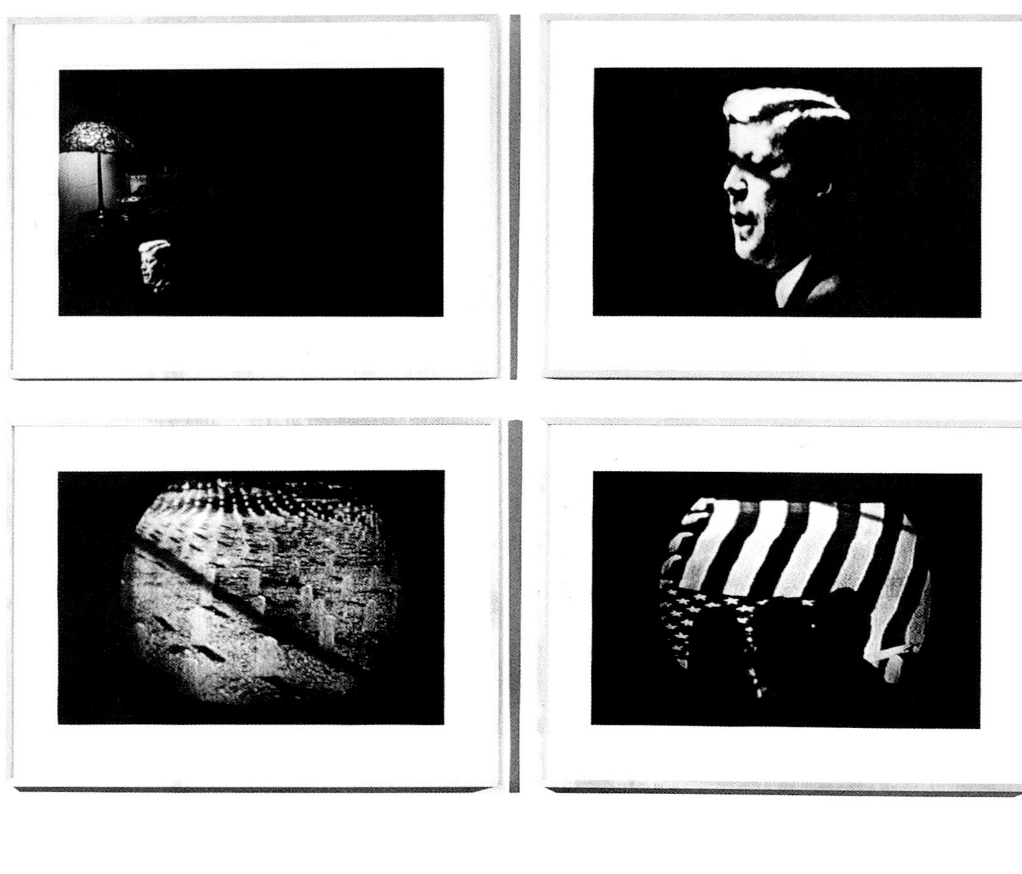

DENNIS HOPPER

Kennedy Funeral, 1963
Suite of eight gelatin silver prints
16 × 24 inches (41 × 61 cm) each
Courtesy of the artist and Tony Shafrazi Gallery, New York

cascaded into homes from November 22 through November 25. We see images of President Kennedy, the caisson that brought his body to Arlington Cemetery, the audiences that witnessed the spectacle, and the U.S. flag. By stilling this flow, Hopper gives the viewer the opportunity to examine closely the images that comprised it—to see their degraded, crudely defined visual properties; to embrace them as electronic images, rather than as material realities; and to question the conflation of the television world with the physical world.

Warhol, too, questioned this conflation in the works he produced in response to the assassination. According to John Giorno, a close friend of the artist's during the early 1960s, the artist's reaction to the assassination and funeral was emotionally wrought. After Giorno learned that President Kennedy had been shot, he went to Warhol's home: "We sat on the Tiffany couch amongst the clutter, watching the live TV coverage from Dallas. We heard Walter Cronkite say, 'President Kennedy died at 2 p.m. on November 22nd, 1963.' We started hugging each other, pressing our bodies together and trembling. I started crying and Andy started crying. We wept big fat tears. It was the symbol of the catastrophe of our own lives. We kissed and Andy sucked my tongue. It was the first time we kissed. It had the sweet taste of kissing death. . . . Everything brilliantly radiated disaster. *'I don't know what it means!'* Andy kept saying in his inimitable voice."[23] Warhol's own account of hearing the news is different. In *POPism: The Warhol '60s*, he writes that he reacted unemotionally when he heard the news over the radio while painting in his studio: "I had been thrilled having Kennedy as president; he was handsome, young, smart—but it didn't bother me that much that he was dead. What bothered me was

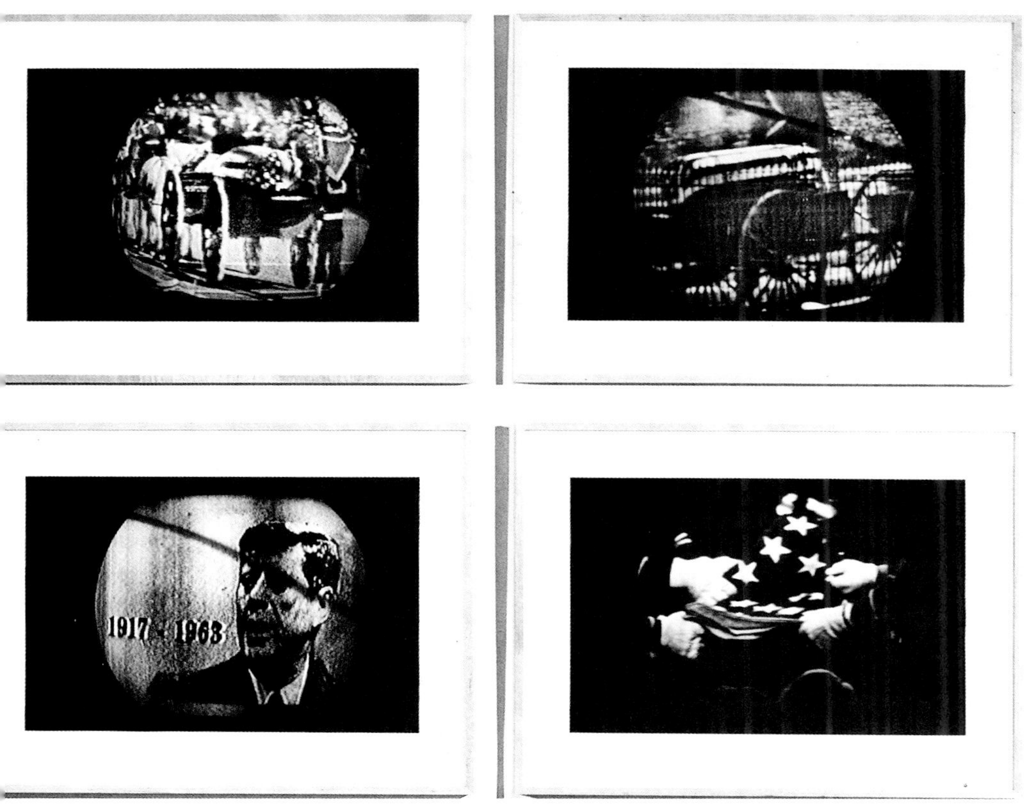

ANDY WARHOL

Flash—November 22, 1963, 1968
(Four prints from the series)
Portfolio, with cover, consisting of eleven serigraphs, plus an additional suite of three
Cover: 22¼ × 21¾ inches
(56.5 × 55.2 cm)
Each serigraph: 21 × 21 inches
(53.3 × 53.3 cm)
The Menil Collection, Houston

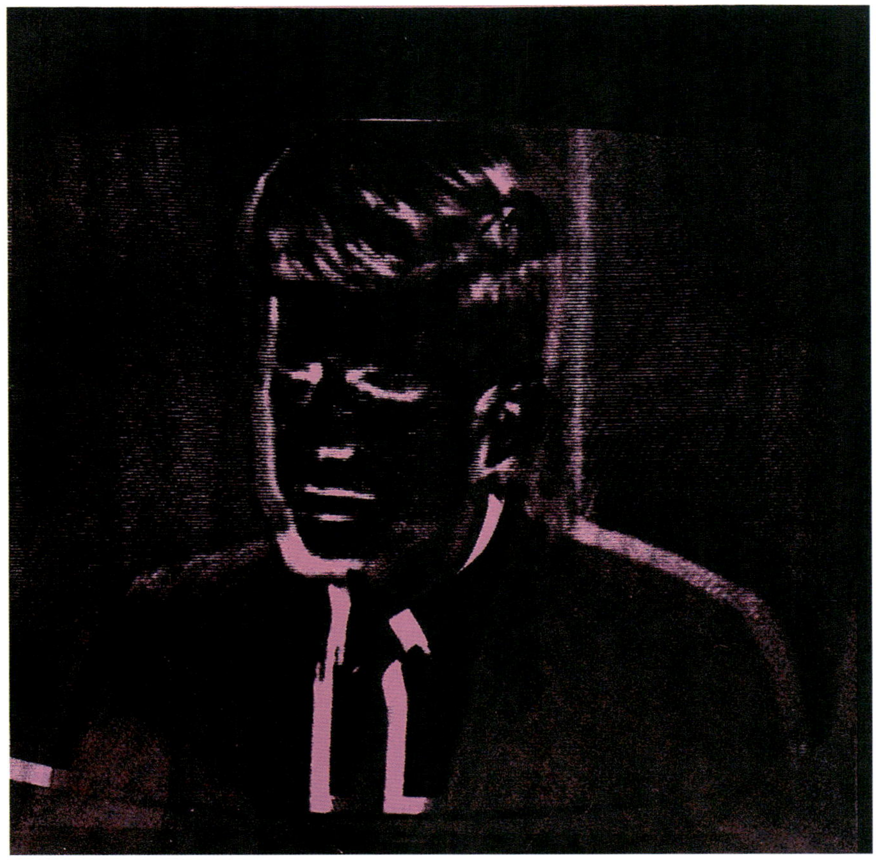

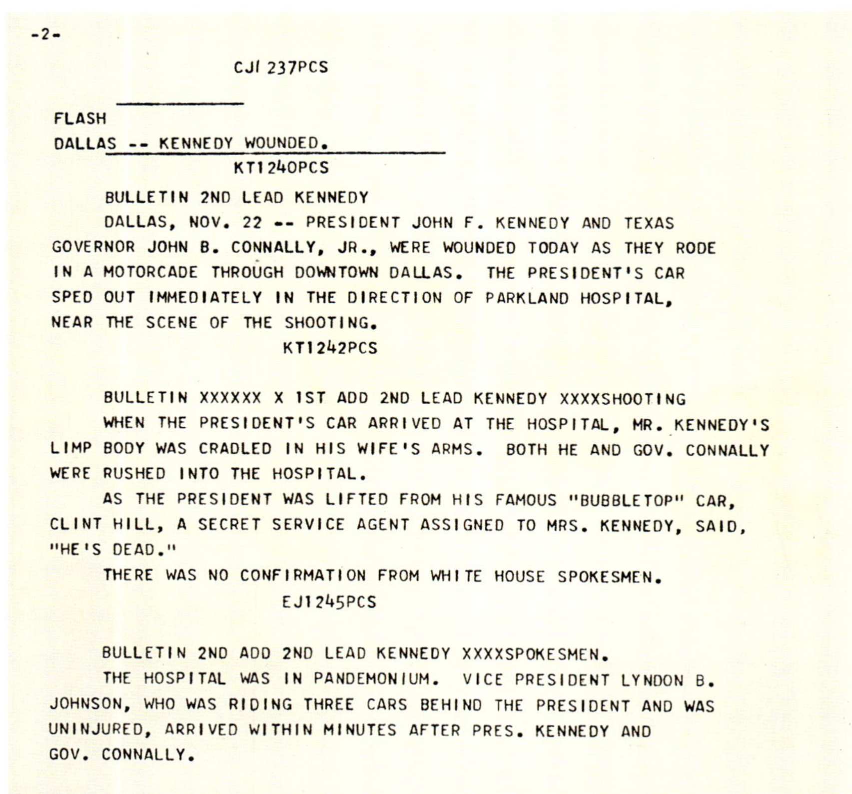

-2-

CJI 237PCS

FLASH
DALLAS -- KENNEDY WOUNDED.

KT1240PCS

BULLETIN 2ND LEAD KENNEDY

DALLAS, NOV. 22 -- PRESIDENT JOHN F. KENNEDY AND TEXAS GOVERNOR JOHN B. CONNALLY, JR., WERE WOUNDED TODAY AS THEY RODE IN A MOTORCADE THROUGH DOWNTOWN DALLAS. THE PRESIDENT'S CAR SPED OUT IMMEDIATELY IN THE DIRECTION OF PARKLAND HOSPITAL, NEAR THE SCENE OF THE SHOOTING.

KT1242PCS

BULLETIN XXXXXX X 1ST ADD 2ND LEAD KENNEDY XXXXSHOOTING

WHEN THE PRESIDENT'S CAR ARRIVED AT THE HOSPITAL, MR. KENNEDY'S LIMP BODY WAS CRADLED IN HIS WIFE'S ARMS. BOTH HE AND GOV. CONNALLY WERE RUSHED INTO THE HOSPITAL.

AS THE PRESIDENT WAS LIFTED FROM HIS FAMOUS "BUBBLETOP" CAR, CLINT HILL, A SECRET SERVICE AGENT ASSIGNED TO MRS. KENNEDY, SAID, "HE'S DEAD."

THERE WAS NO CONFIRMATION FROM WHITE HOUSE SPOKESMEN.

EJ1245PCS

BULLETIN 2ND ADD 2ND LEAD KENNEDY XXXXSPOKESMEN.

THE HOSPITAL WAS IN PANDEMONIUM. VICE PRESIDENT LYNDON B. JOHNSON, WHO WAS RIDING THREE CARS BEHIND THE PRESIDENT AND WAS UNINJURED, ARRIVED WITHIN MINUTES AFTER PRES. KENNEDY AND GOV. CONNALLY.

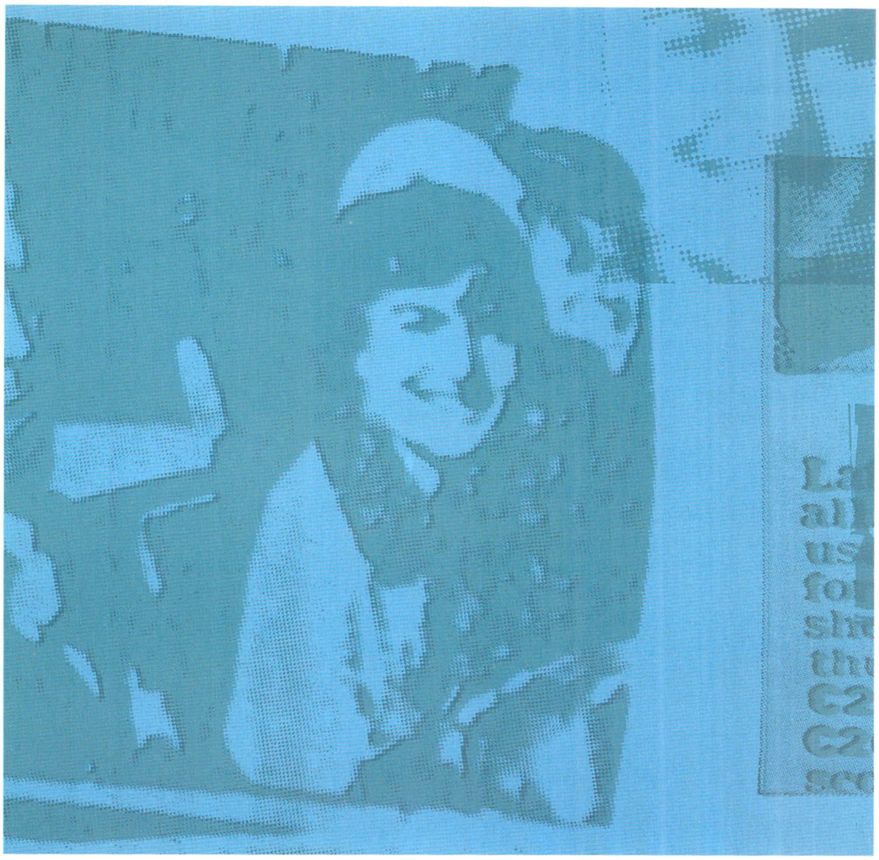

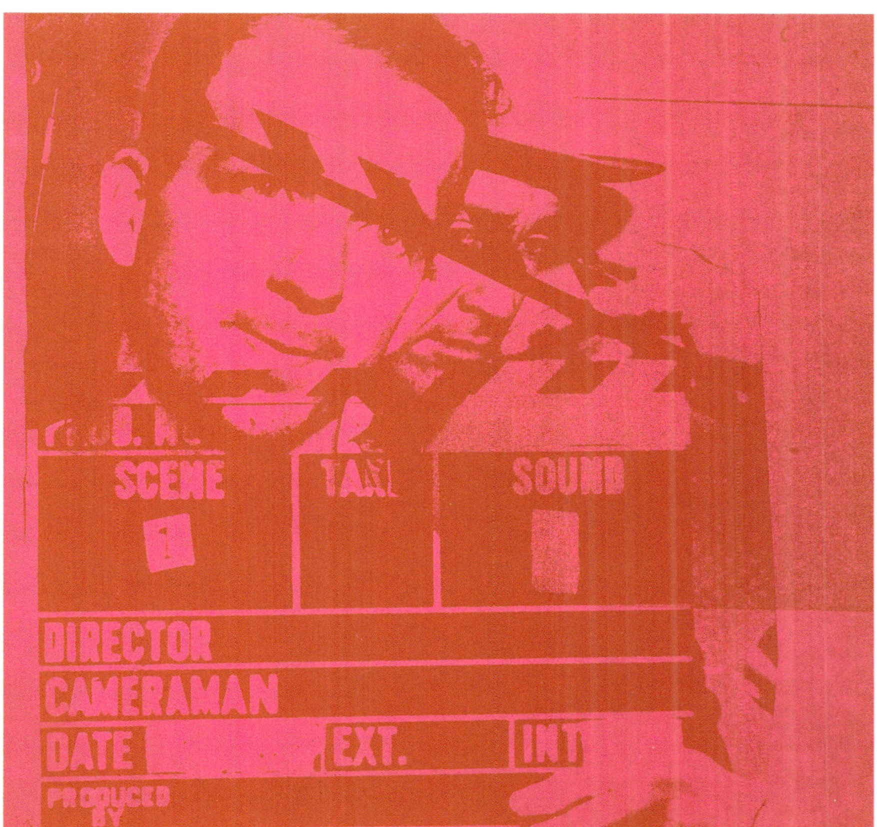
SCENE
1
SOUND
DIRECTOR
CAMERAMAN
DATE
EXT.
PRODUCED BY

BRUCE CONNER

TELEVISION ASSASSINATION
1963–64/1975
8mm film (black and white, silent),
Zenith television set with painted
screen, Bolex film projector,
film reel, and electric cord
Television: 15½ × 21 × 13½ inches
Projector: 9 × 3½ × 5½ inches
Collection Walker Art Center, Minneapolis;
Gift of Robert Shapazian, 1992
(not included in this exhibition)

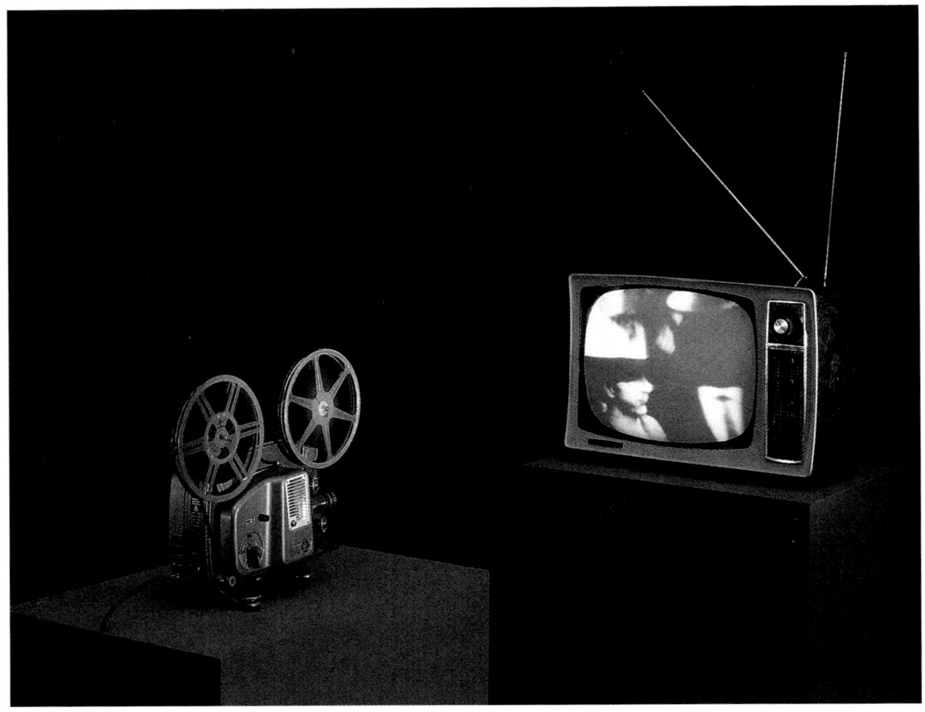

the way television and radio were programming everybody to feel so sad. It seemed like no matter how hard you tried, you couldn't get away from the thing."[24] In this plainly stated lament, Warhol seems to define the emotional reality of the President's death as an effect of the media barrage it sparked.

Even though he professed to be annoyed by the manipulation of the media, Warhol produced a variety of works based on media images in response to this experience. In 1963–64, he made a series of silkscreen paintings consisting of groups of 20-by-16-inch panels featuring single photographic images of Jacqueline Kennedy. In addition, he produced several screenprints using the same images in 1965–66; an artist's book with twelve screenprints, supplemented by a suite of three, entitled *Flash—November 22, 1963*, in 1968; and an unfinished film in the late 1960s.

Warhol's decision to focus on the image of Jacqueline Kennedy, the perfect complement to the Television President, was strategic, because the proliferation of her image in the media had transformed her into a celebrity: a woman whose identity dissolved into the images that circulated in the mass media. Warhol himself understood this, as his cynical remark that Jacqueline Kennedy's "performance" during

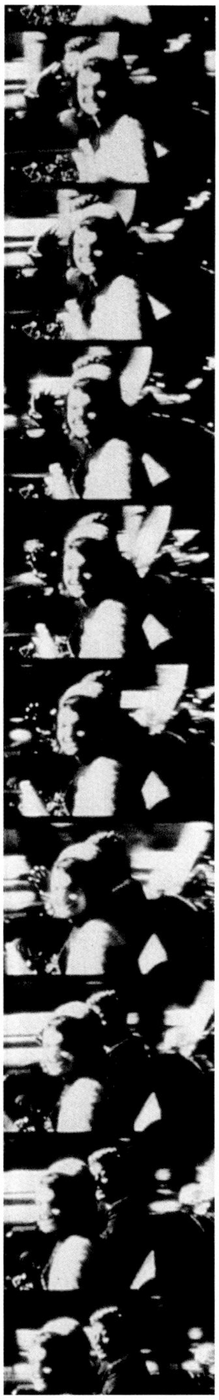

BRUCE CONNER

Opening images of *REPORT. A Film by Bruce Conner*, 1963–67
(detail from filmstrip)
16mm film, black and white, 13 minutes
Print Courtesy of Bruce Conner and Canyon Cinema

the Four Dark Days was "the best thing she's ever done!" suggests. The sources of the images he used for the Jackie panels are eight photographs reproduced in popular magazines like *Life* and *Look*, as well as newspapers, which he cropped to focus on Jacqueline Kennedy's face. He silkscreened these photographs onto single canvases of rectangular and circular format and released many of the resulting paintings as single-panel works. He also produced several multipanel works by arranging groups of the single panels into grids. As in Rauschenberg's silkscreen paintings, the original magazine photographs from which Warhol derived these images are clearly focused, while the images as they are rendered in the paintings themselves are not. Self-consciously mediated, these images display the low definition of the televisual rather than the printed photographic image. And instead of signifying painting's relentless drive toward self-purification, their dissolution into flatness suggests the static of electronic transmission, as the real is transformed into images broadcast on the television screen and then projected onto the pictorial surface. Moreover, Warhol's transformation of the photographs mimics the technical strategies of televised coverage of the assassination—especially its use of close-up and repetition—which the networks used to intensify viewers' emotional involvement with, and to accentuate the perceived realness of, the televised images. Finally, the sequencing of the panels creates a discontinuous narrative that implies the presence of television by evoking its broadcasts of film and video of the Kennedys in the hours and minutes before the assassination with images from the live feeds of its aftermath, images that were broadcast over and over during the Four Dark Days. In summary, Warhol's compulsive repetition of images of Jacqueline Kennedy in these panels, which exist in resonance with their repetition on television, can be read as a drive to negate the reality of a singular death that television made emphatically real through the continuity, immediacy, and visuality of its coverage. The authenticity of this reality was indexed by the emotional response that it elicited in many viewers, who were programmed, as Warhol poignantly revealed through the works themselves and through his words, to feel so sad.

Like Warhol, Bruce Conner was disturbed by television's coverage of the assassination and its aftermath. Between 1963 and 1967 Conner produced eight versions of a thirteen-minute, black-and-white film entitled *REPORT* that used actual footage from the networks' coverage. In his film installation *TV ASSASSINATION*, he projected a version of this film onto an actual television set, its screen painted white. Like Warhol, Conner was affected by television's annexation of President Kennedy's death as a means of legitimating its own cultural authority as a producer and purveyor of the

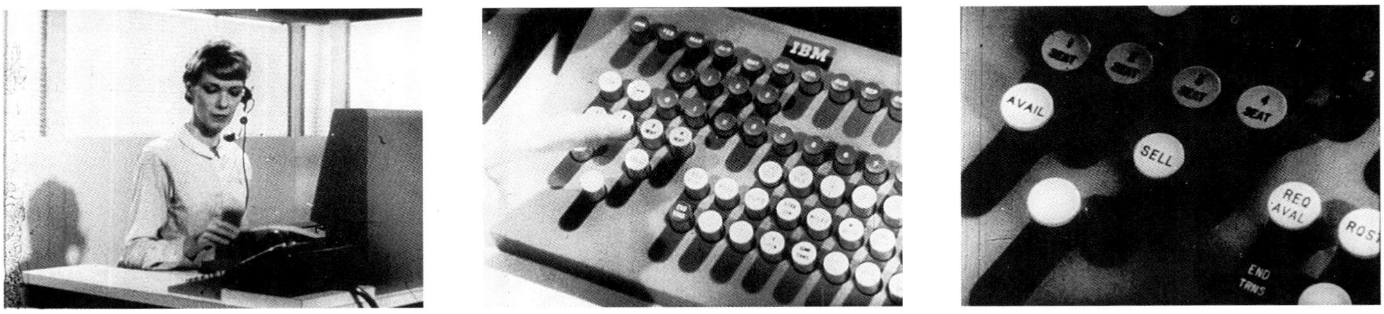

BRUCE CONNER

Final images of *REPORT, A Film by Bruce Conner.* 1963–67 (film stills)
16mm film, black and white, 13 minutes
Print Courtesy of Bruce Conner and Canyon Cinema

real. However, while Warhol merely lamented the viewer's inability to escape the influence of the deluge of images that flowed forth from television, Conner was repelled by television's exploitative transformation of the absolute reality of death into spectacle: "When I started [to make *REPORT*] the big problem was that I had to show what had happened: the exploitation of a man's death. . . . It's what I wanted to show and I had to show it because nobody else was. There was tons of other information coming through the media—but this exploitation was the most obvious thing to me. . . . The problem in making the film was that in order for me to do the film I would also have to go through this same process that those people were using to exploit Kennedy. If the film was completed he was as dead as they had made him and so it took me 2 ½ years to finish the film. That has something to do with why it changed. Part of the reason that it changed was I didn't want to stop the change . . . like life is change and when *REPORT* was finished then he was dead. So it took 2 ½ years for me to acknowledge that he was dead."[25]

The first version of *REPORT* is a brief 8mm film that Conner began making immediately after the assassination by shooting coverage directly from the television screen. The other versions are 16mm films that he made that incorporate this footage as well as 16mm footage he purchased commercially. In addition, these versions include footage he purchased of seemingly unrelated events, such as a bullfight, the mad scientist in his laboratory in *The Bride of Frankenstein*, children climbing fences, a lightbulb being shattered by a bullet, an atomic bomb explosion, the erection of power lines, film leader, and other footage. The soundtrack, which is not synchronized to the images, consists of a radio announcer describing the events preceding and following the assassination. Although the eight versions of the film that Conner ultimately produced adhere to essentially the same structure, he recombined the footage in a manner reminiscent of his collages and

ANDY WARHOL

Jackie, 1964
(Four paintings from the series)
Silkscreen ink on synthetic polymer paint on canvas
20 × 16 inches (50.8 × 40.6 cm) each
The Andy Warhol Museum, Pittsburgh
Founding Collection, Contribution The Andy Warhol Foundation for the Visual Arts, Inc.

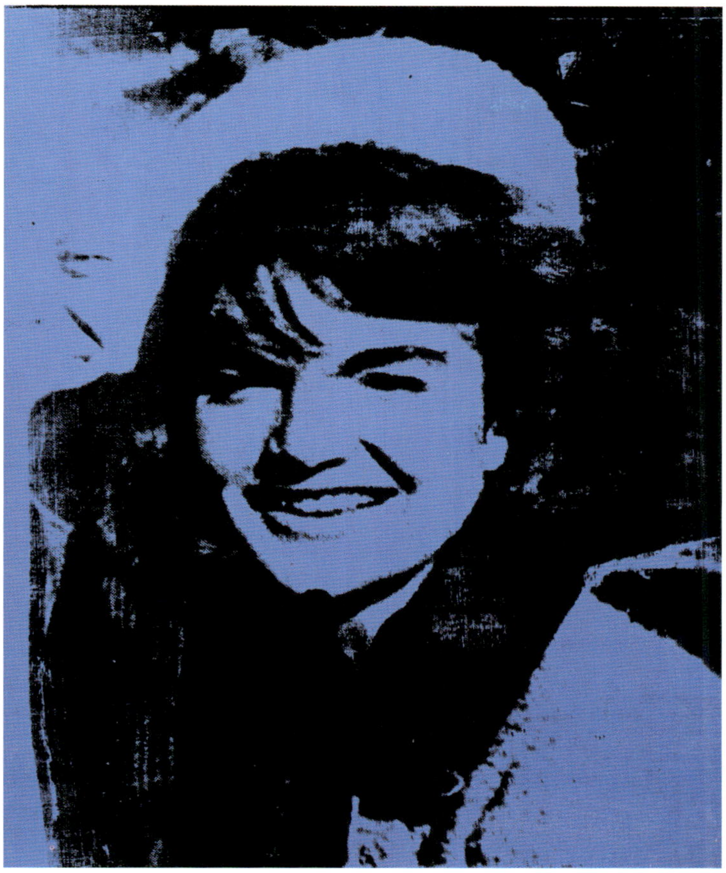
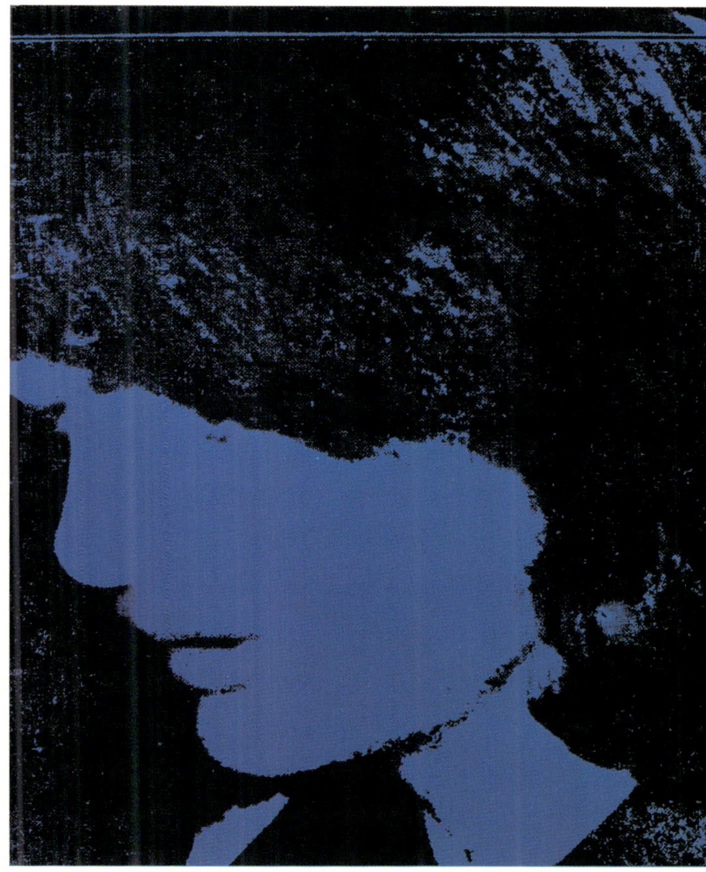
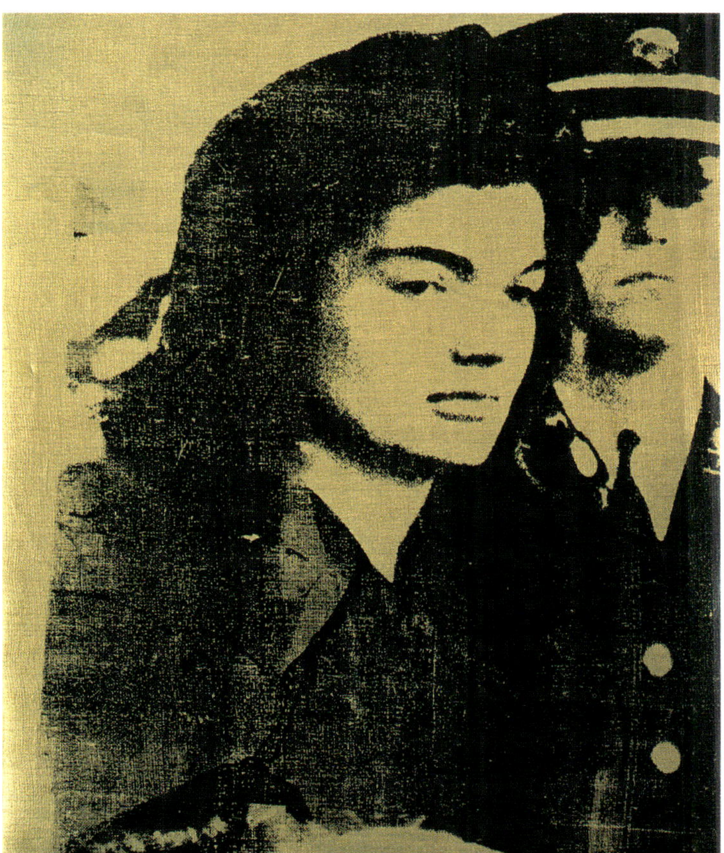
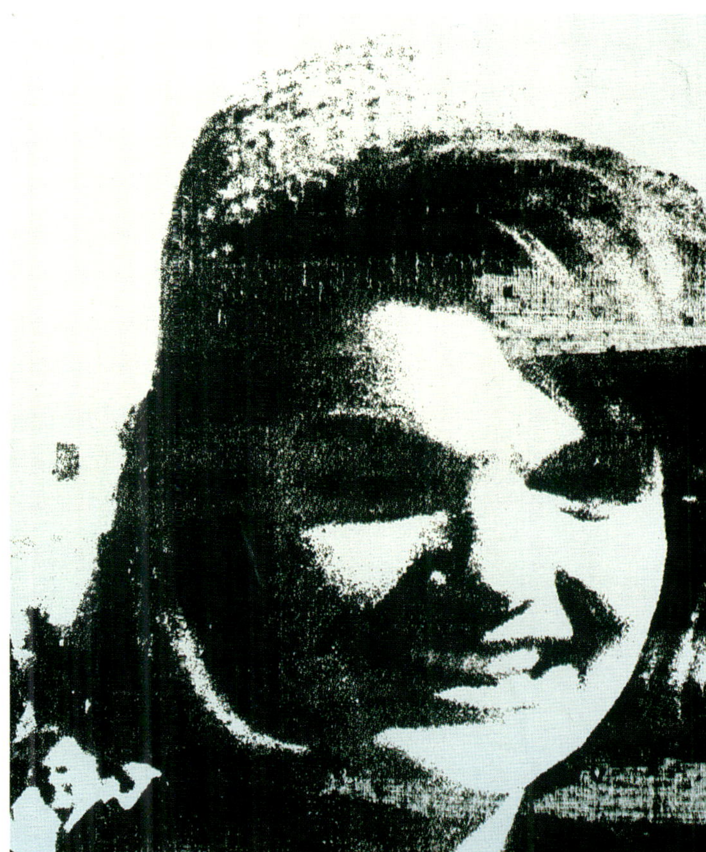

assemblages. The fact that *REPORT* exists in eight versions implies that there is no single, authoritative truth, as truth is inevitably modulated by its continual transformation in the televisual flow. Conner denaturalizes the experience of watching this flow by deforming it—by repeating, accelerating, slowing down and stopping, and strategically juxtaposing the images that constitute it. The film's final shot is a close-up of a switchboard operator at the Stock Exchange pressing a button labeled "SELL." Epitomizing Conner's criticism of broadcast coverage of the assassination as "the exploitation of a man's death," this image underscores his perception of the extent to which television, as a point of exchange within a circuit of power, effectively consumed the lived reality of death, transforming it into a spectacular commodity.

Coda: Pop People

In 1965, *Tape Recording* magazine invited Warhol to experiment with some of the first videocameras available on the U.S. market: a Norelco slant-track video recorder, a remote-control television camera with a zoom lens, and a Concord MTC 11 hand-held videocamera with a Canon zoom lens. With this equipment he made two thirty-minute tapes of Edie Sedgwick—one of his "Superstars," who appeared in several of the films he shot at his studio called "The Factory"—as well as several other tapes. He incorporated the tapes of Sedgwick into *Outer and Inner Space* (1965), his first double-projection film. On both projections, Sedgwick sits in front of a television

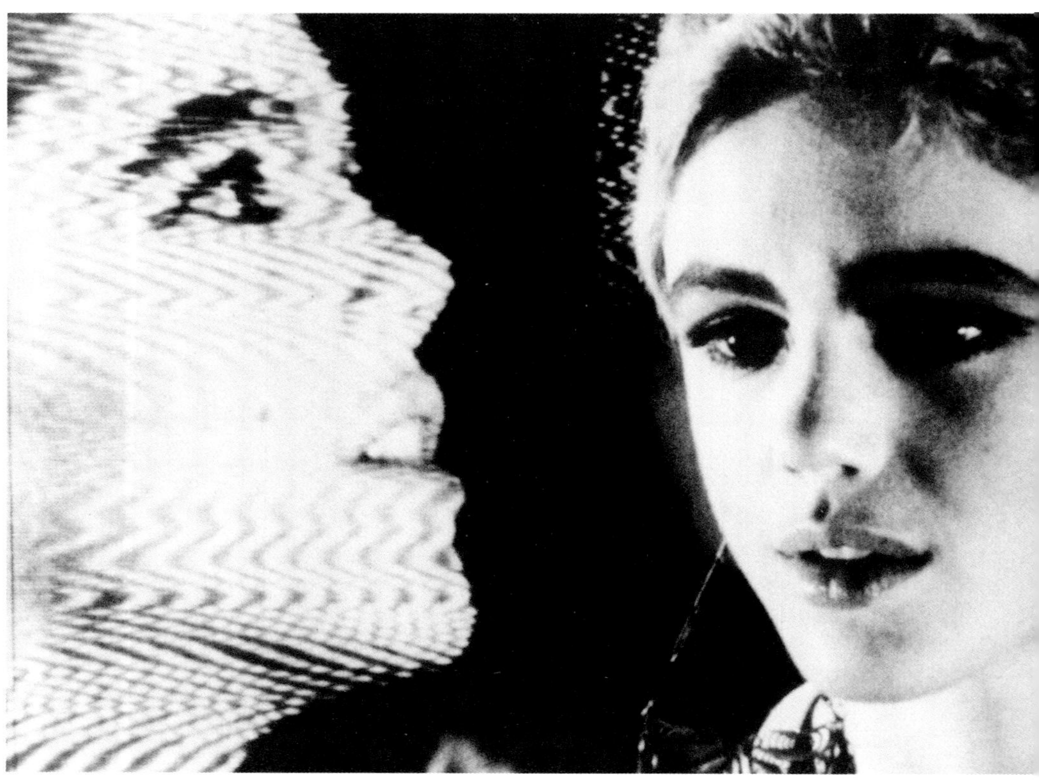

ANDY WARHOL

Outer and Inner Space, 1965
(film stills) 16mm film, black and white, sound, transferred to video, 33 minutes, double screen
The Andy Warhol Museum, Pittsburgh

set that is playing the videotapes that Warhol shot: a close-up of her glamorous face accentuated by her dangling earrings; she talks nonstop about nothing for the duration of the tape. While the filmed image captures her visage in grainy tones of black and white, the taped image is in a process of constant deformation, alternately dissolving her face into mobile zigzag lines, doubling it with wavering ghost images, and voiding it into blackness. As the film progresses, Sedgwick becomes more and more disturbed by the image of herself that she sees on the television screen. When she sees herself sneezing, for example, she becomes noticeably disoriented and begins sneezing in awkward syncopation with the taped image. And as she says at one point, "It makes me so nervous to listen to it." It makes the viewer uncomfortable, too, to witness this spectacle of a woman coming undone as she confronts her image on television.

In *Outer and Inner Space*, Warhol presents the confrontation between the television world and the material world, between the image and the real: the binary oppositions that television itself had begun to undo as it paved the way toward the new frontier of the hyperreal. As the cultural theorist Douglas Kellner observed, "In this universe, we enter a new form of subjectivity, in which we become saturated with information, images, events, and ecstasies. Without defense or distance, we become a 'pure screen, a switching center for all the networks of influence. . . .' In the media society, the era of interiority, subjectivity, meaning, privacy, and the inner life is over; a new era of obscenity, fascination, vertigo, instantaneity, transparency, and overexposure begins."[26] Welcome to the new frontier, Pop People.

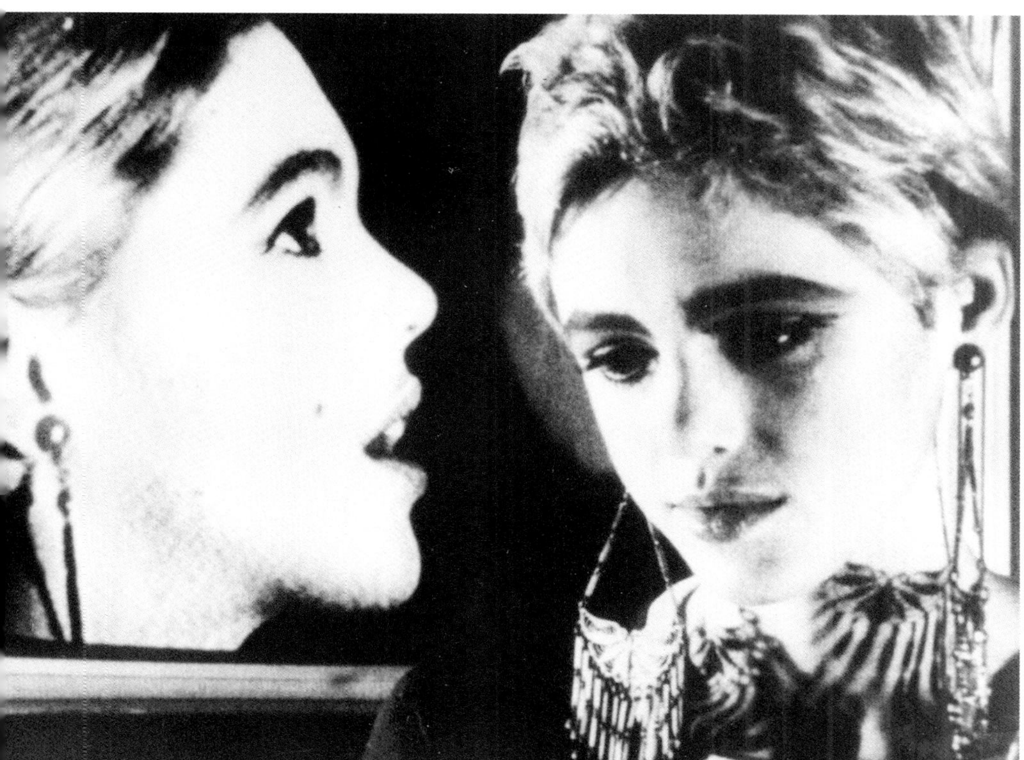

Notes

I would like to thank Benjamin H. D. Buchloh and Jonathan Crary, the advisors to my dissertation, "Art into Television, 1960–65," Columbia University, New York, 1998, which inspired this project. I would also like to extend my sincere thanks to Elizabeth Ferrer for the opportunity to create an exhibition based on my research and to acknowledge Lisa Dirks, Dana Friis-Hansen, Naomi Sawelson-Gorse, and Gail Sanders for perspicacious comments on this essay, which improved it greatly. In addition, I would like to thank John Alan Farmer M.D. and Elizabeth Walker, and also Luong Ly, for their support.

1 It was during this acceptance speech that Kennedy first used the term "New Frontier" to describe his political vision for his presidency—a vision based on his commitment to searching for forward-looking solutions to the problems that the country faced.

2 Address of the Honorable John F. Kennedy accepting the nomination for the Presidency of the United States from the official proceedings of the Democratic National Convention 1960, pp. 239–244.

3 Marshall McLuhan, *Understanding Media: The Extensions of Man* (New York: Mentor, 1964), p. 276.

4 Ibid., pp. 272–73.

5 Ibid., p. 33.

6 Ibid., p. 280.

7 As has now been well established, the reception of Dada during this period resulted from a nexus of concrete events. The 1951 publication of Robert Motherwell's *The Dada Painters and Poets: An Anthology*, which was read by many artists, was seminal. Also important were one-person exhibitions of the works of important figures such as Marcel Duchamp, Kurt Schwitters, and others, as well as group exhibitions such as *Dada 1916–23*, organized by Duchamp and presented at Sidney Janis Gallery in New York from April 15 to May 9, 1953; and *Dada: Dokumente einer Bewegung*, which opened in Düsseldorf in September 1958 and then traveled to Frankfurt and Amsterdam. Several movements that emerged in the 1950s and 1960s were indebted to Dada in various ways. Pop: an international movement that emerged in the mid-1950s in England and later in the United States and other countries in which artists began to engage with postwar consumer culture by producing works that, often ironically, drew from the mass media, including magazines, newspapers, film, television, and advertising. For more information, see Marco Livingstone, *Pop Art*, exh. cat. (London: Royal Academy of Art, and Weidenfeld + Nicolson, 1991). Fluxus: a loosely defined international movement that emerged in the early 1960s. Although its definition is hotly contested, Fluxus artists were (and still are) interested in questioning conventional conceptions of art, the artist, and the art object. In their efforts to reconnect art and life, they often used materials from everyday life to create objects, actions, or events, often located outside of art institutions, that contested the status quo. For more information, see *In the Spirit of Fluxus*, exh. cat. (Minneapolis: Walker Art Center, 1993). Assemblage: a medium that became prevalent in the late 1950s in which artists used everyday objects as the basis for works of art. For more information, see William Seitz, *The Art of Assemblage*, exh. cat. (New York: The Museum of Modern Art, 1961).

8 For a more detailed discussion of the emergence of the Neo-Dada avant-garde, see *Neo-Dada: Redefining Art 1958–62*, exh. cat. (New York: The American Federation of Arts in association with Universe Publishing, 1994), with essays by Susan Hapgood, Maurice Berger, and Jill Johnston.

9 Andy Warhol, in John L. Wasserman, "Conjurer's Dream from Pop World," *San Francisco Chronicle*, May 23, 1966, p. 52.

10 Rosetta Brooks, in *Kienholz: A Retrospective*, exh. cat. (New York: Whitney Museum of American Art, 1996), p. 86.

11 Lynn Spigel, *Make Room for TV: Television and the Family Ideal in Postwar America* (Chicago: University of Chicago Press, 1992), p. 50.

12 Robert Rauschenberg, in Barbara Rose, *Rauschenberg* (New York: Vintage Books, 1987), p. 72.

13 Andy Warhol, *The Philosophy of Andy Warhol (From A to B and Back Again)* (New York: Harcourt Brace Jovanovich, 1975), p. 26.

14 Of this series, Rosenquist has stated: "The middle painting with the two figures and the boat [*TV Boat 1*, 1966] might almost be like a figure painting for some people. Originally they were all going to have titles of towns or small cities in the U.S.: Waco, Texas; Mobile, Alabama; Aspen, Colorado; Fargo, North Dakota. Four cities like rear projection beauty, like everyone is watching television or some communication; then these can be named cities, as locations. If the location of all the people watching is poured into a broadcasting television station of some kind, then the illustration of the broadcast could be a city. It's like inside-out." Rosenquist, quoted in Gene Swenson, "Social Realism in Blue," *Studio International*, February 1968, cited in *James Rosenquist*, exh. cat. (Valencia: Centre Julio González, 1991), p. 203.

15 For a more detailed discussion of the televisual properties of Rauschenberg's silkscreen paintings, please see my dissertation, "Art into Television: 1960–65," Ph.D. diss., Columbia University, New York, 1998, pp. 64–125.

16 Dean Swanson, *Robert Rauschenberg: Paintings, 1953–1964*, exh. cat. (Minneapolis: Walker Art Center, 1965), unpag.

17 Mason Klein, "'To be sad, because I was once a child': The Collages of Ray Johnson," in *Ray Johnson: Correspondences*, ed. Donna De Salvo and Catherine Gudis, exh. cat. (Columbus: Wexner Center for the Arts, The Ohio State University, and Paris: Flammarion, 1999), p. 51.

18 The following description is synthesized from photographs by Rolf Jährling, Manfred Leve, George Maciunas, and Manfred Montwé, and textual accounts by Maciunas and Tomas Schmit. Schmit's account is the most extensive: see Tomas Schmit, "exposition of music," in *Nam June Paik, Werke: Musik—Fluxus—Video*, exh. cat. (Cologne: Kölnischer Kunstverein, 1976), pp. 67–71. Paik himself published four texts in various Fluxus vehicles that mention the exhibition: "Exposition of the Music," *dé-coll/age*, no. 3 (December 1962); an untitled text in the brochure accompanying the exhibition, which also includes a text by Jean-Pierre Wilhelm; "New Ontology of Music," published in Paik's *Monthly Review of the University for Avant-garde Hinduism* (1963); and "afterlude to the EXPOSITION of EXPERIMENTAL TELEVISION," *fLuxus cc fiVe ThReE*, no. 4 (June 1964). Reviews of the exhibition include: John Anthony Thwaites, "Der Philosoph und die Katze," *Deutsche Zeitung*, April 9, 1963; Siegfried Bonk, "Über dem Eingang ein blutiger Ochsenkopf: Nam June Paik in Galerie 'Parnass,'" *Kölner Stadt-Anzeiger*, March 16–17, 1963; *NRZ an Rhein und Ruhr, Wuppertaler Stadtnachrichten*; Wolf Schön, "In Neo-Dadas Kindergarten: Erste Begegnung mit der Kunst aus der Mülltonne," *Rheinischer Merkur*, March 16, 1963; Zett, "Absurder Klamauk am Abgrund: Eine 'Musikausstellung' in Rolf Jährling's 'Parnass,'" *Westdeutsche Rundschau*, March 15, 1963; and F.v.B., "Peinlich-steriler Blödsinn," *Westdeutsche Rundschau*, date unknown (a response to Zett). Copies of all but Thwaites are available in The Gilbert and Lila Silverman Fluxus Collection.

19 Wolf Vostell, "television dé-coll/age for millions 1959," in Vostell, *dé-coll/age happenings*, trans. Laura P. Williams (New York: Something Else Press, 1966), p. 12.

20 Ernst Dichter, *The Strategy of Desire* (Garden City, N.Y.: Doubleday and Co., 1960), p. 92.

21 Vance Packard, *The Hidden Persuaders* (New York: David McKay and Co., 1957), p. 31.

22 "America's Long Vigil," *TV Guide*, January 25–31, 1964, p. 20.

23 John Giorno, "Andy Warhol's Movie *Sleep*," in *In a Different Light: Visual Culture, Sexual Identity, Queer Practice*, eds. Nayland Blake, Lawrence Rinder, and Amy Scholder, exh. cat. (San Francisco: City Lights Books, 1995), p. 200.

24 Andy Warhol and Pat Hackett, *POPism: The Warhol '60s* (New York: Harcourt Brace Jovanovich, 1980), p. 60.

25 Bruce Conner, in "Bruce Conner," *Film Comment* 5 (Winter 1969), p. 18.

26 Douglas Kellner, *Jean Baudrillard: From Marxism to Postmodernism and Beyond* (Stanford: Stanford University Press, 1989), p. 72.

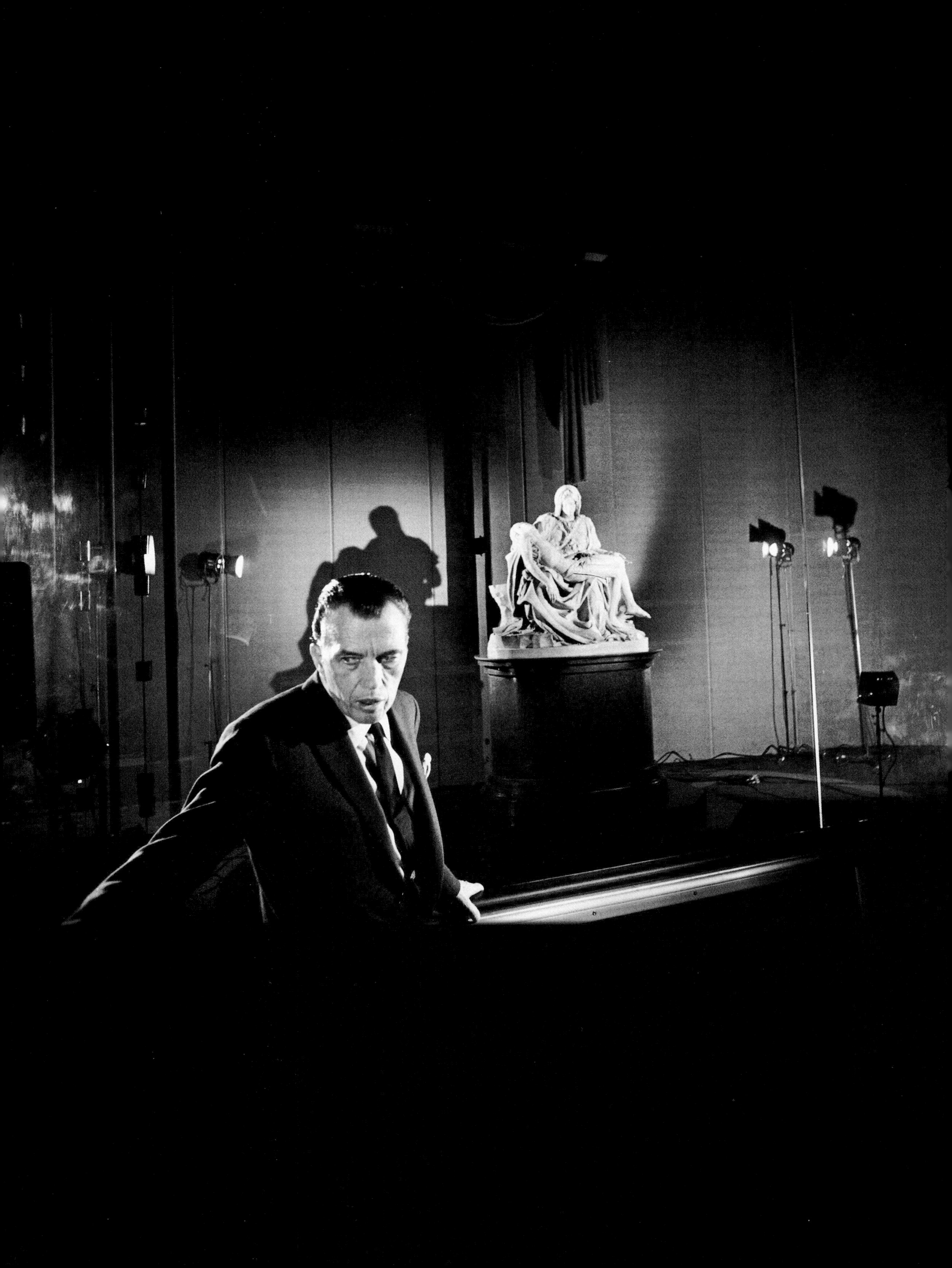

sound bites & spin doctors

NAOMI SAWELSON-GORSE

Museums, educational institutions, art and slick magazines and newspapers deserve much of the credit for stimulating the new interest in art.
—Irving Sandler, "In the Art Galleries," *New York Post* (December 10, 1961)

He should have added television.

Saturday, January 2, 1960

The penultimate day of a long weekend.

For a few, the next class of their "Outlines of Art History" college television course. While most New Yorkers were still asleep, these tube-students awoke before dawn, turned on their TV sets, tuned into the local CBS channel, readied their pads and pens, and studiously took notes while watching a pre-recorded tape of New York University art history professor Jane Costello's lecture "Gothic Art in Italy" from 6:30 to 7:00 a.m., in the series appropriately named *Sunrise Semester*.[1]

For some, a pause while flipping through the pages of the just-issued weekly *TV Guide* to peruse a feature story about Brian O'Doherty—Irish expatriate, former medical doctor, now a painter, poet, Harvard graduate, and since 1958 a local television celebrity. In his *Invitation to Art* series of half-hour programs telecast from Boston's Museum of Fine Arts on that city's educational station, WGBH, "O'Doherty gives Boston viewers an offbeat look at art," so the magazine's readers are informed, by "comparing Sam Snead's golf swing to the artist's brush strokes in a Manet masterpiece ('Both men display ease and perfection of style')."[2]

Ed Sullivan with Michelangelo's *Pietà* at the Vatican Pavilion during the 1964 World's Fair in New York. Television had originally premiered at the 1939 World's Fair in New York.

"New Approaches to the Old Masters," *TV Guide* (Minnesota ed.), January 2, 1960, p. 16.

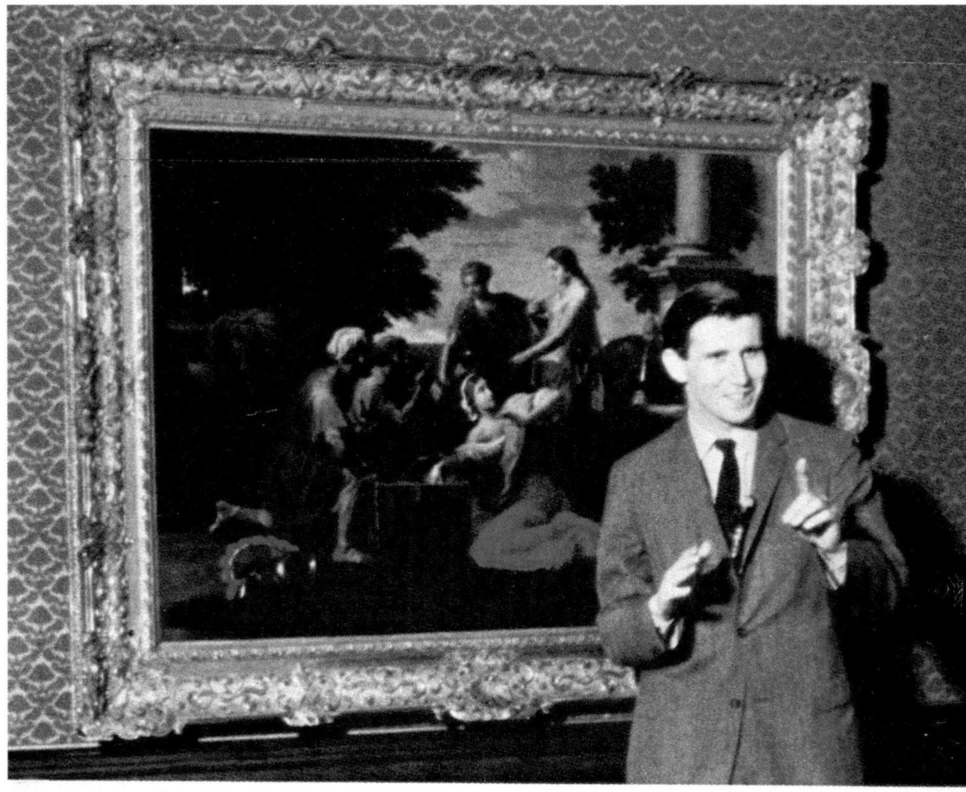

NEW APPROACH TO THE OLD MASTERS

Brian O'Doherty gives Boston viewers an offbeat look at art

By comparing Sam Snead's golf swing to the artist's brush strokes in a Manet masterpiece ("Both men display ease and perfection of style"), Dr. Brian O'Doherty has made art devotees out of many Bostonians.

Dr. O'Doherty makes such comparisons on his *Invitation to Art* series, telecast from Boston's Museum of Fine Arts over WGBH-TV, an educational-TV station. The series is being kinescoped for the National Educational Television and Radio Center for distribution next fall to educational-TV outlets in the United States.

The doctor quit medical practice in his native Ireland three years ago for graduate work at Harvard—in psychology. An artist of some note, he stayed in America to paint, write poetry and talk about art on TV.

Discussing Da Vinci's "Mona Lisa," O'Doherty may remark: "Women's smiles are ambivalent. Women don't know what they want. Men must make up their minds for them." Pointing out the realism of still-life works by Melendez, he says: "You can almost pick the banana off the canvas" —and does. Among the paintings he'd planted a bogus canvas bearing a real banana.

16

Others might take a look at *TV Guide*'s blurb on the adventures awaiting John Viyvan as "Mr. Lucky" on his floating casino *Fortuna* that evening from 8:00 to 8:30 on CBS: "Mr. Lucky is very puzzled when a war-time buddy sends a hideous painting as a birthday present, months before his birthday. Lucky's curiosity is further aroused by the artist's violent attempts to get the painting back."

Meanwhile, television viewers are apprised that at a news conference that day, the Democratic Party's junior senator from Massachusetts, John F. Kennedy, officially announced his run for the presidency.

In the days that followed, viewers could eschew the increasing dialogue on the tube about the race for the presidency by opting to watch a superabundance of telecasts that were billed as entertainment. Quite a few incorporated art in one way or another into their plotlines, characters, even overall themes. At least five aired on the evening of Sunday, January 3, 1960. They ran the gamut of typical fare: a made-for-TV bio-drama, a Western, a detective story, a Hollywood movie, a teleplay. Beginning in the prime-time slot of 7:00 p.m. was *Sunday Showcase*'s "The Margaret Bourke-White Story," featuring Teresa Wright as the acclaimed *Life* photographer whose career ended with the advent of Parkinson's disease, with Bourke-White herself making an appearance at the program's conclusion. Then came *Bat Masterson*'s dandified lawman and professional gambler "who believes that a painting purchased by his friend Teresa Renault is real, and he backs up his opinion with a large wager." Its one-hour time slot intruded on another channel's telecast of the 1949 Hollywood movie *The Fountainhead*, starring Gary Cooper and based on Ayn Rand's best-selling novel, which *TV Guide* summarized as a story about an "unconventional architect" who "struggles to maintain his personal integrity." The movie's running time overlapped another channel's episode of *Bourbon Street Beat* with its lead detective, Rex Randolph, hired by art gallery owner Sybil Dole to find a stolen painting. And ending the evening, just shy of midnight, was a rerun of *Command Performance*'s "The Intolerable Portrait," about an art critic's search for a "deliberately hidden portrait" by a famous artist whose biography he is just completing.

Art's tube-image in these opening days of 1960 was predominantly white, wealthy, and upper-class. Its messenger sometimes female. Its acclaimed artists mostly male. There were those who painted, photographed, or designed buildings; those who promoted as critics, educators, and dealers; those who amassed as collectors and connoisseurs. The artist who could no longer work; the artist who refused to work; the artist as a bizarrely crazed almost-felon. An artist's brush likened to a golfer's nine iron. Ancient relics. Medieval art. Religious art. Realistic art. Abstract art. Modern and contemporary art. Valuable works. Fakes and forgeries.

The art market as a dubious site of swindlers, thieves, and gamblers. Archaeological digs. Homes that housed art collections. Universities as promoters; museums as endorsers; corporations as sponsors. Art as instructional; art as entertaining; art as thrill-seeking; art as normative.[3]

mixed media demographics

Although only fifty or sixty viewers enrolled for credit with New York University in Jane Costello's "Outlines of Art History," the *New York Times* reported that the overall audience was almost 120,000—an astonishingly high figure for a not-for-prime-time educational art program broadcast to a limited regional market.[4] Perhaps her audience was similar to Brian O'Doherty's Boston-area viewers who, he noted, came "from all walks of life," and whose experience of art was minimal. Their interest was stimulated by his use of everyday language, which included sports metaphors along with his self-professed "raconteuring, enthusiasms, satire and irony."[5] In fan mail he received, O'Doherty noticed how "many . . . make a particular point of saying that they know nothing about art, but they know that they like the program. Most letters are from the same people who watch Ed Sullivan and 'Gunsmoke.'"[6] A typical, yet intriguing, demographic that mixed vaudeville acts with Western gun-slinging heroes, gussied up with a dab or so of art, for entertainment.

Aline Saarinen would soon encounter a similar audience. Hired in 1962 as the first art critic to appear regularly on a network daily program, and as one of a handful of women on national network television in a high-profile, on-camera capacity, Saarinen hosted eight-minute segments that usually aired every two weeks on NBC's *Today* show. These segments made art part of the program's formulaic offerings and her a nationwide television celebrity. She, however, loathed the term "art critic" as her designation on *Today*. Suitable for print media, she said, but inappropriate on television because it "sounds so stuffy." If television "should be entertaining," Saarinen argued, then getting the stuffiness out of art was essential if it was to become not only normative tube fare but also "a natural part of [the] daily lives" of viewers. Taking down art's "sacred cows," using vernacular language instead of art-historical jargon, and finding similarities between athletics and art imagery were some of the ways in which she sought to dispel art's elitism.[7]

If her fan mail was any indication, audience reactions to her approach seemed to prove her success. Their comments were, however, markedly different from the ones

O'Doherty received. While his devotees admitted to liking his program as much as they liked Westerns and variety shows, Saarinen's admirers focused predominantly on her gender. Some would profess voyeurism, complete with scatological allusions and sexual innuendoes—as when an unnamed "professor" informed her of leaving "the bathroom door open" so that he could watch her "while he's shaving," to which Saarinen remarked, "It's such fun to catch them unawares!" With *Today* airing nationally from 7:00 to 9:00 a.m., when most perform their early morning daily routines, Saarinen provided bathroom banter, at least for some. For others, she would delineate her viewership in gender stereotypes that she herself faced as a woman, mother, and recent widow of Eero Saarinen, the Finnish architect who designed CBS's national headquarters building in New York: "Here on 'Today' you get men shaving in motels, women doing their housework."[8]

Perhaps Jane Costello encountered a similar audience. Perhaps she was taken unawares. In the first months of 1960, when the *New York Times* noted her as a local tube celebrity, she was very much a novice about all things television. Before her initial appearance in the fall of 1959 for her first semester of "Outlines of Art History," Costello confessed that she had never owned a television set.[9] She was in the minority of the U.S. population. As of May 1959, only 14 percent of households could say the same, while 78 percent owned one set, and 8 percent two or more. Near the end of the Eisenhower administration, television was ubiquitous. As the foremost popular cultural institution, it had replaced movie houses and front porches as the primary site of entertainment and social interaction. The population had turned inward, to their living rooms, to watch programs—sometimes in hushed silence, sometimes with shared guffaws, sometimes while eating TV dinners. Television, which supplanted family chatter around the dining-room table, had become the hearth of the domestic dwelling. By 1960, the appetite to own a boob-tube continued to increase: 88 percent of the 44 million U.S. households owned at least one set. Five years later, in 1965, a swelling and more affluent population had added more sets to its homes, with 20 percent having two or more, while a scant 8 percent were without any.[10]

Beginning in the fall of 1960, some of those millions of households had the chance to see O'Doherty on their local stations. His engaging tube-image, along with the national publicity he was receiving in publications such as *TV Guide*, led to the national distribution of his *Invitation to Art* series among approximately sixty-four educational television outlets, with some networks also picking it up. His program was not unique in attracting nationwide attention from the ever-increasing audience for art. However, for some programs, the lag time between development and national airing could take years, as it had for *Sunrise Semester*, even though it was immensely popular locally. To encompass television's demographic was to understand its diversity: what was a sure sell in New York City might bomb in Carson City—or vice versa.

These differences highlighted art's television dilemma. A program host's tube-image, as well as the format of the program itself, had far more to do with saleability and commercial appeal to viewers than the program's content per se. While networks and sponsors placed merchandising and entertainment above education as the purpose, goal, and format of anything on television, the majority of the producers involved in promoting art on the medium argued the reverse. Their logic went something like a media axiom: Any art telecast was a natural sell since art and television were both visual, and once color was widely introduced and made affordable, art could be relished on the tube in all its splendor. To them, art on television was a happy marriage of mixed media.

It was a contention that had a long history in television's brief life. In October 1939, when the artist Charles Sheeler was interviewed on New York's newly established NBC television station to promote his retrospective at The Museum of Modern Art (MoMA), he reportedly exclaimed: "It may even be that television has brought us to the threshold of another Renaissance in the visual arts" because "television will do for art what the radio has done for music!"[11] Such a juxtaposition—likening radio's success in reaching vast audiences to television's potential to do the same for the visual arts—was a utopian prophecy for art's certain and unlimited achievement on television.[12] But on the tube, nothing was secure, a natural sell, or wedded bliss. Especially for elitist art. "Art as the tabernacle of the sacrosanct" might sell well to cognoscenti, but for the majority of the television audience, it "is a bore," quipped O'Doherty.[13] And downplaying art's snobbery was what he and Aline Saarinen attempted to accomplish.

and now a word from our sponsor

Playing up art's elitism lay elsewhere in TV-land, most especially in television commercials, to which the term "art" was applied frequently as a moniker. Among the many instances was a half-hour program called *Cavalcade of Spots* that originated at a Los Angeles station and consisted entirely of advertisements. The station's president at once defended and applauded the program's concept and content by pointing out "that some of the most creative material on television today is contained within the commercials."[14] His viewpoint was sanctioned not only by the advertising industry's own self-promoting accolades for the best television ads, but also by The Museum of Modern Art, the most renowned modern art institution in the United States. In 1963, MoMA's first retrospective of television programming, *Television U.S.A.: 13 Seasons*, surveyed programs and commercials broadcast between 1949 and 1961 that the organizers thought notable for historical or aesthetic reasons. With this exhibition, MoMA validated not only the status of the medium itself as a fine art, but also the commercials that appeared on it, as many newspapers and magazines were quick to point out. Asserted one headline: "TV Commercials Can Please, as Well as Sell, Museum of Modern Art Show Proves."[15]

Aesthetically alluring, iconographically complex, illusionally rich, diverse in form and content, these advertisements—"in a medium that puts a high premium on art"—differed dramatically from their "high" model, *Newsweek* told its readers: "not art for art's sake, not art that delights or enlightens, but art that sells cars, cigars, plane tickets, stomach remedies, and savings accounts." By 1965, when a television-commercial festival was held at New York's avant-garde film theater, the Bleecker Street Cinema, some of the best tube ads were spoken of reverently as *Gesamtkunstwerk* (total work of art), usually "outclassing the programs they interrupt."[16] An example is a commercial for Band-Aids—its imagery eerily akin to a cinematic rendition of a Giorgio de Chirico *scuola metafisica* or a Max Ernst surrealist painting—that *Newsweek* likened to films by Stanley Kubrick, François Truffaut, and Alfred Hitchcock: "A little girl, hardly more than a baby, races along an endless beach, alone in the vast world. . . . Is she fleeing from terror or running toward hope? . . . But what does it mean? The answer comes suddenly: the child . . . holds up her index finger, and cries: 'Mommy!'"[17]

While ads like this one often aesthetically outclassed their sponsored programs, they more frequently outclassed art programs themselves, at least according to MoMA. Among the numerous telecasts to be included in *Television U.S.A.*'s "The Arts and Sciences" section, only one was an art program, "Family of Man" (from the science-oriented educational series *Adventure*), which took its title and subject from MoMA's 1955 exhibition organized by its director of photography, Edward Steichen. Other art-related telecasts in the exhibition addressed history (such as an interview with Western classical scholar Edith Hamilton in the series *Wisdom*), or technique (as with *Camera Three*'s "Waiting for Krazy" and "The Stamp of Steinberg," about cartoons and cartoonists).

The exhibition omitted any other art programs sponsored by numerous museums.[18] Although the cover of the catalogue featured Ben Shahn's 1953 serigraph, *Calibans*, the only other nod to the subject was a pithy history of early art telecasts by former CBS executive Gilbert Seldes. Seldes had helped New York's Metropolitan Museum of Art and other area art organizations to promote themselves and their collections on the air through his network. Like MoMA, these museums used television to publicize their institutions as they promulgated their own art-historical canon (under the umbrella of education) to a large audience that would, they hoped, lead to increased attendance.[19]

However, a "new frontier of culture" was emerging in network programming, as one television critic noticed.[20] For almost a decade, the Federal Communications Commission had required networks to set aside a specific number of hours for public affairs and/or educational telecasts to raise the level of what all agreed was program mediocrity. But the networks conformed to the requirements by consigning public affairs and educational telecasts out of prime time, where mediocrity was standard fare. When Newton Minow became the Kennedy-appointed FCC chairman, he vigorously pursued the networks to alleviate this situation. He termed network television "a vast wasteland"—a sobriquet for the tube's barren programming contents, that was so compelling that it long outlived Minow's own brief tenure on the FCC.[21]

As a way to satisfy FCC requirements and to partially address Minow's epithet for television, the networks devised a special sales pitch, which they termed "corporate image." Contrived to entice companies to finance what seemed then a losing proposition, corporate image was, in essence, cultural payola. As one newspaper explained it, an "advertiser wants to dignify his concern by associating it with a quality show." But the bottom line of such dignity was money. If advertisers allocated the majority of their television advertising budget to pay for costly commercials to air on high-rated, prime-time shows, sponsoring public affairs or cultural specials seemed like a bargain, or so went the sales pitch of one network's "sponsor-hunter." As he stated: "So they come to us, and they can buy a show that gives them prestige, commendation from critics and public officials and, most important, they won't have anything left over in their budget."[22] For networks who sought sponsors who in turn sought corporate image, art on television was pin-money that filled network coffers while balancing company accounts.

For Minow and his FCC colleagues, however, corporate-image programming was far from sufficient to counteract the networks' general disinclination to offer more quality shows. While the networks sought to attract corporate sponsors, the FCC pushed to increase the number of outlets for cultural programming by proposing federal funding for educational series, establishing a national education network, and outfitting every TV set with UHF (ultra-high frequency) channels. Did these steps result in the banishment of art to the limited telecasts of public television and a reduction in art programs offered by the networks? Yes and no. The plethora of art-based plotlines that riddled television programs in early January 1960, for example, had diminished. In the meantime, art issues were incorporated into many segments of news broadcasts as well as end-of-the-year wrap-ups. In television's vast wasteland, art was not an outcast; it had become news.

and now the news: Mona Lisa & Baseball

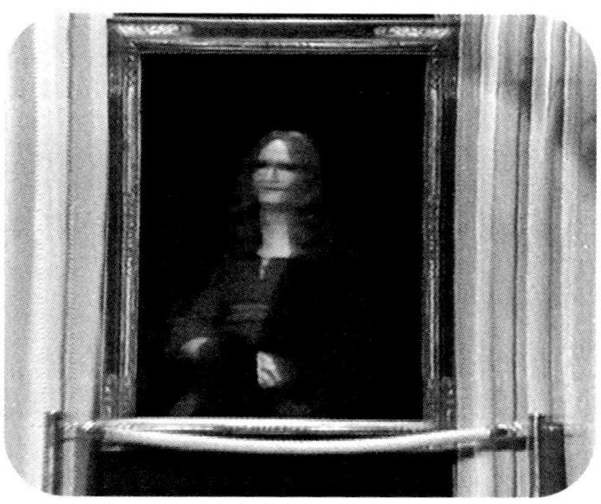

Steve Allen as the *Mona Lisa* in the opening skit "The Shtick Museum of Art," on *The Steve Allen Show*, rebroadcast on November 28, 1963.

When two trucks passed each other in opposite lanes of the New Jersey Turnpike on February 4, 1963, this daily occurrence was seen by one television network as far more than coincidental: it was "a cultural sign of our times."[23] Thousands had queued up to catch a glimpse of the trucks' contents, which television ballyhooed as cultural icons of all things American and all things Italian Renaissance: James Whistler's *Arrangement in Grey and Black, No. 1* (familiarly known as *Whistler's Mother*), en route for display at Atlanta's High Museum; and Leonardo da Vinci's *Mona Lisa*, traveling from its initial viewing at Washington, D.C.'s National Gallery of Art to the Metropolitan Museum of Art for its next showing.

Both paintings were on loan from the Louvre, with the *Mona Lisa* making its U.S. debut. The work had, in fact, made its debut earlier—on television—on *The Steve Allen Show*. Allen's on-set audience had no trouble recognizing the painting, or the other replicated artworks featured in an opening skit, "The Shtick Museum of Art," which re-aired during the height of *Mona Lisa* mania. After the camera scanned works that elicited immediate identifications from the audience—Thomas Gainsborough's *Blue Boy*, Grant Wood's *American Gothic*, as well as *Whistler's Mother*—its lens rested on closed curtains. As they parted, audience howls greeted Allen in drag as "Lisa Gioconda, wife of Big Frank Giocondo," complete with her famous "Candid Camera" smile and crossed hands around her waist (because she was in "handcuffs"). Yet another new fact was then told to the audience: though his subject was dressed, Leonardo had painted her as a fold-out "centerpiece for *Playboy*" magazine.

Skits like Allen's satiric tableau vivant—with all of its ethnic barbs and gender stereotypes—provided "easy laughter, which never did anyone harm," and were unlikely "to alter art's unquenchable pride," stated one art critic.[24] Certainly they did not diminish art's audience—whether television viewers, museum and gallery goers,

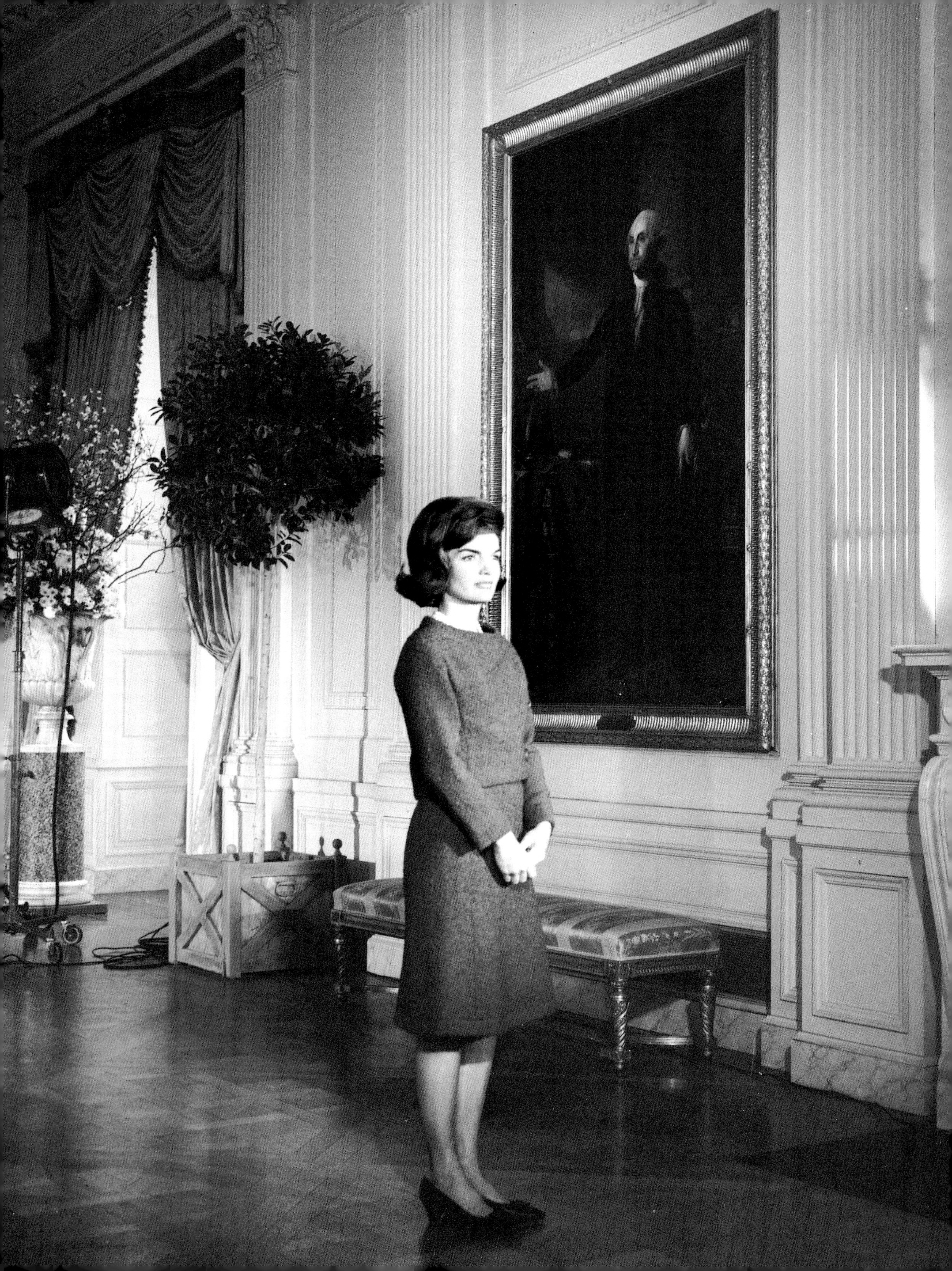

Jacqueline Kennedy during the taping of "A Tour of the White House with Mrs. John F. Kennedy" (CBS, February 14, 1962).

auction bidders and art book buyers, or television viewers watching museum and gallery goers and auction bidders and art book buyers. In this postwar era, art had become collective as well as popular knowledge. In fact, art banter was so ubiquitous that, said Marcel Duchamp, "Art has become a thing like baseball."[25] By 1963, museums had replaced baseball as the great American pastime in attendance.[26] (Sidebar: in 1962, Andy Warhol would make silkscreen paintings featuring repeated images of both the *Mona Lisa* and a baseball player).

Television, as a common carrier of culture, had democratized both art and itself. Art was no longer the purview of elitism at colleges, museums, galleries, and auction houses. One did not have to physically travel to see art, walk among ancient ruins, stroll through museum corridors, listen to an artist's lecture or hear a round-table discussion of critics at an educational or art institution. Television, which attempted to blur distinctions among its diverse demographic, similarly merged space, time, and locale. For art, television ultimately realized André Malraux's "museum without walls"; every TV set in every home served as art's carrier, venue, information source, and interpreter.[27] Beginning in 1962, *Telstar* and other communications satellites would bring immediacy to time-delayed broadcasts when the Louvre and the Acropolis were shown in real time in living rooms in the United States. (Meanwhile, in the first *Telstar* telecast on July 23, European viewers saw a baseball game as their opening vision of the United States.[28])

The Jackie Look

On April 9, 1960, some viewers got the chance to see a rerun of the 1953 episode of *I Love Lucy* when Lucy "becomes a sculptress." In order to promote latent artistic talent in her yet unborn child, Lucy takes up sculpture at the prodding of a shady art supplier and dealer. In turn she deceives an art critic, who believes she is the world's next Michelangelo. Television stereotypes about the art market, represented either as heroes or swindlers, had arisen as early as the medium's debut in 1939. In the 1950s, these conventions became more embellished due to the increasing commodification of art that arose from postwar economic prosperity, a burgeoning and more educated middle class, and baby-boomer parents who wanted to keep up with the Joneses. During the Kennedy administration and the first years of the Johnson presidency, when art was sanctioned by governmental approval and new federal agencies, had a more visible national presence on television, and was enhanced by the introduction of color telecasts, the former stereotypes of connoisseurship and swindle now became emblematized as knowledge and money. Gone was the ditzy dame as art's sucker played by Lucille Ball, among others, in the 1950s.[29] Jacqueline Kennedy had transformed that. If her husband's tube-image had assisted him in securing the presidency, then her tube-image would raise the profile of art in becoming the nation's new pastime.

She, for one, would not be the victim of a scam, or so she told the millions of television viewers who accompanied her and Charles Collingwood on a tour of the White House on the evening of February 14, 1962. The committee overseeing its refurbishing was carefully scrutinizing every donation to assure authenticity, worth, and appropriateness. Tacitly, all understood that such intense examinations of contributions were necessary because Jackie wanted only "the best" in order to make the White House "America's cultural showcase."[30]

Jackie had attended the National Gallery of Art's twentieth-anniversary celebration the previous March, her first television appearance since the inauguration. She was present again for the capital's debut of the *Mona Lisa*, which her husband spoke of reverently as "the work of one of the greatest figures of the greatest Western age of creativity."[31] And when the series *Accent* did its overview of the important events of 1961, "Accent on 1961: A Public Memoir," and proclaimed the Kennedy era as the greatest age of interest in creativity in the history of the United States, she was there, too. Hers was the nation's "new look" of motherhood and keeper of the cultural hearth—as was sung in calypso tempo accompanied by a bongo drum by a member of Seven Come Eleven's parodying troupe:

> . . . Learn to sew
> Learn to cook
> Learn to read Italian from a book
> Don't have a weary look or a wacky look
> But a look they're calling The Jackie Look
> Got to be chic
> Got to be smart
> Got to learn a lot about modern art . . .[32]

Television offered its viewers ample programming from which to learn not only about art, but also that art itself was a fiercely contested issue. For example, one episode of producer David Wolper's syndicated show, *The Story of . . .*, featured contrasting assessments of the works of avant-garde artist Ed Kienholz. While the *Los Angeles Times* art critic Henry Seldis dismissed the artist's work as having "no aesthetic value

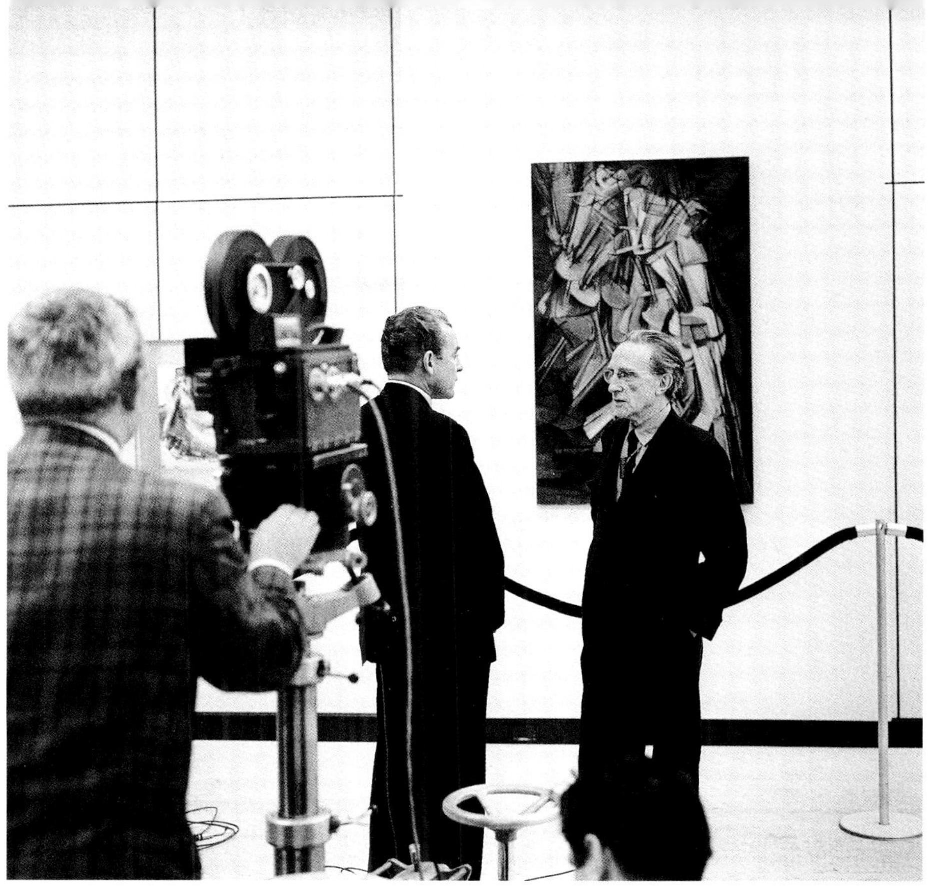

Charles Collingwood interviewing Marcel Duchamp for the *Eyewitness* program, "The Art Show That Shocked America" (CBS, aired on April 5, 1963).

whatsoever"—a comment that inspired Kienholz to produce his 1961 assemblage *The Big Eye (Homage to H.S.)*, which incorporated the chassis of an actual television set—*Arts & Architecture* art critic Dore Ashton considered his work to be an "inspired and authentic commentary on contemporary society." On *The Nation's Future*, broadcast on June 3, 1962, there was a truculent debate between Thomas B. Hess, executive editor of *Art News*, and John Canaday, art critic for the *New York Times*, on the validity of modern and contemporary art, especially Abstract Expressionism. During a 1963 CBS telecast of *Eyewitness* about the 1913 Armory Show re-creation, "The Art Show That Shocked America," the audience was perhaps as confused as moderator Charles Collingwood when his questions to Kenneth Clark, art dean of British television and museum director, elicited erroneous facts and xenophobic prejudices about the history of twentieth-century modern art as they toured the exhibition. The subsequent film segment of Collingwood's more intriguing dialogue with Marcel Duchamp about his infamous painting, *Nude Descending a Staircase, No. 2*, the Armory Show's *cause célèbre*, was so edited down that Duchamp's remarks became mere sound bites.

Just two years earlier, on December 13, 1961, *David Brinkley's Journal* aired a report on the newest trends in French art with works by Arman, Raymond Hains, and Niki de

Saint Phalle, that was linked with a segment about paintings done by children and chimpanzees. These old stereotypes of modern and contemporary art were, apparently, not at all worn out.[33] Nevertheless, they were beginning to give way, though not without skepticism. Government sponsorship of the arts, rarely discussed seriously since the W.P.A. projects of the Depression era, became one of the most hotly debated topics on television. Whereas Jackie Kennedy demurely refused to reply to Collingwood's query on this subject during the White House tour telecast, president-appointed Special Consultant on the Arts August Heckscher frequently fielded questions on this issue during numerous telecasts. When on February 12, 1965, a month before Lyndon Johnson would ask Congress to pass legislation establishing the National Foundation on the Arts and Humanities, ABC—perhaps unwittingly, surely coincidentally—aired "The Forgotten Man," a program in its *F.D.R.* series, in which Ben Shahn discussed the W.P.A. program and its importance to cultural life in the United States. Without a doubt, in this heyday of the Kennedy era's highbrow culturalization, the United States was "on a culture kick," searching for an artistic heritage so that the country would claim, stated Heckscher, "its place in history . . . not alone by its military or economic power, but by the quality of its civilization."[34]

Saturday, January 2, 1965

For most, the penultimate day of a long weekend.

For some viewers, a chance to see a time-delayed broadcast of NBC's *Year End Review*, which included Aline Saarinen's wrap-up of art events.

On Monday, these same viewers could watch the two mid-morning series simply titled *Architecture* and *Antiques*; or, on Tuesday, during the late evening, another episode in *Artist Series*. Earlier, in the mid-afternoon, they might have opted to see Art Linkletter's *House Party* with painter and art gallery director Richard McKenzie, who would judge "housewives' portraits" of the show's host. Wednesday brought a rerun of an episode from the early 1960s series *Thriller*, with mystery writer Beatrice Graves purchasing "a strange painting that has brought violent death to several of its previous owners." On Friday, Saarinen's *Today* segment focused on a New York City children's art gallery. And in the subsequent week, *Eye on New York* featured avant-garde art with sculptor George Segal and collector Robert C. Scull, while *My Living Doll* had an episode with its main character, Rhoda, copying a Picasso "right down to a perfect forgery of the signature."

The previous May, industry statistics had estimated that the "average family" watched television for more than five hours per day.[35] It is not known how many saw any of the numerous programs airing that month about the reopening of The Museum of Modern Art, which CBS newscaster Mike Wallace called "an event that made cultural history."[36] In the opinion of Claire Beach, Washington, D.C.'s local WTOP television reporter, this event marked a different milestone. To her, the rededication of the museum by Mrs. Lyndon Johnson was "her first and strongest bid to succeed Mrs. John Kennedy as a cultural leader." After Lady Bird "pressed the switch," illuminating "the completely renewed citadel of modern art" to the joyous throng of invited guests, the First Lady declared that "the battle to enrich the nation's cultural life is just as important as the war against the poverties of man's necessities."[37] However, Lady Bird couldn't and wouldn't become art's TV messenger as her predecessor did—though she would narrate ABC's tour of Washington, D.C., pointing out plans for its redevelopment and beautification.[38] Ada Louise Huxtable, architecture critic for the *New York Times*, noticed the dramatic change shortly after President Johnson's first State of the Union address:

> In the Kennedy years, the air was charged with a sophisticated vitality that brought . . . electric life . . . and serious artistic ambitions. . . . Now all this is being transformed. The glitter is gone, the preoccupation with beauty no longer holds top priority, and the emphasis has shifted from culture to welfare. Talk is of the human condition, rather than of the esthetic tradition.[39]

Soon, the human condition would become the nation's paramount consideration, because of television.

When Marya Mannes reported in 1965 that National Education Television was "going full steam ahead for next year, with a series of programs for the nation's educational stations on contemporary trends in American art," Barbra Streisand was making plans for her second television special at the Philadelphia Museum of Art, while Gene Kelly had already obtained permission to do his dance number in The Museum of Modern Art's sculpture garden.[40] CBS was working on a number of news specials about Paul Gauguin, Henry Moore, the "Wyeth Phenomenon," and the art of the 1960s; NBC rejoined with programs attempting to define Americanism through artworks at the Whitney Museum of American Art. Meanwhile, Saarinen would be increasingly engaged as the network's correspondent on matters other than art, including Vietnam, now acknowledged as TV's first war.[41] ■

Notes

My thanks to John Alan Farmer for inviting me to mull over art on TV, Moira Roth for providing numerous segues and introductions, David Joselit for connections, Michelle Deziel for musings, and G.L.G. for giving time. For their generous assistance in unearthing archival and video recording materials, I am indebted to Judy Throm and Barbara Bishop of the Archives of American Art; Amy Garawitz and the staff of the Museum of Television and Radio's Los Angeles office; Steve Wilson and Linda Ashton of the Harry Ransom Humanities Research Center at the University of Texas at Austin; Susan K. Anderson of the Philadelphia Museum of Art; Karen Lucic of Vassar College; Bonnie Clearwater of the Museum of Contemporary Art in North Miami; Mary K. Coffey of Pomona College; Michelle Elligott of The Museum of Modern Art, New York; the Interlibrary Loan department at Honnold Library of the Claremont Colleges; and the staff at UCLA's Film and Television Archive.

1 Every two weeks, tube-students taking the course for college credit would meet Costello at the university for a two-hour class. See John P. Shanley, "Art Class At Dawn," *New York Times*, February 7, 1960, sec. 2, p. 13. *Sunrise Semester*, which began airing in 1957, was produced by New York University in cooperation with the local CBS television station in New York and was a "pioneer in college-credit courses on television," according to Val Adams, "News of TV And Radio: 'Sunrise Semester' To Be Shown Over C.B.S. Network," *New York Times*, June 23, 1963, sec. 2, p. 17.

2 "New Approach To The Old Masters," *TV Guide* (Minnesota ed.), January 2, 1960, p. 16. O'Doherty would eventually host more than seventy *Invitation to Art* programs on WGBH-TV. Unless otherwise noted, all program times noted are Central Time and all information and quotations about television programs are taken from the Minnesota regional *TV Guide*; the *New York Times* television listings; Daniel Einstein, *Special Edition: A Guide to Network Television Documentary Series and Special News Reports, 1955–1979* (Metuchen, N.J.: Scarecrow Press, 1987); *Three Decades of Television: A Catalog of Television Programs Acquired by the Library of Congress, 1949–1979*, ed. Sarah Rouse and Katharine Loughney (Washington, D.C.: Library of Congress, 1989); Tim Brooks and Earle Marsh, *The Complete Directory to Prime Time Network and Cable TV Shows, 1946–Present (Sixth Edition)* (New York: Ballantine, 1995); and the holdings of the Museum of Television and Radio.

3 For critical analysis of television stereotypes and typologies, see the seminal essay by Lynn Spigel, "High Culture in Low Places: Television and Modern Art, 1950–1970," in *Disciplinarity and Dissent in Cultural Studies*, ed. Cary Nelson and Dilip Parameshwar Gaonkar (New York and London: Routledge, 1996), pp. 313–46, which argues that the "history of art on television is bound up with ideas about nationalism, race, xenophobia, and threatening sexualities that the medium both constructed and proliferated" (p. 315); and Karel Ann Marling's chapter on "Hyphenated Culture: Painting by Numbers in the New Age of Leisure" in *As Seen on TV: The Visual Culture of Everyday Life in the 1950s* (Cambridge, MA: Harvard University Press, 1994).

4 Shanley, "Art Class At Dawn."

5 "New Approach to the Old Masters," p. 16.

6 Brian O'Doherty, "Art on Television," in *The Eighth Art: Twenty-Three Views of Television Today* (New York: Holt, Rinehart and Winston, 1962), p. 111.

7 "Frank Views on Art (Including Sacred Cows) Are Offered By Critic Aline Saarinen On NBC-TV's 'Today,'" and "Aline in Wonderland," NBC news releases, February 13 and 27, 1963, Eero and Aline Saarinen Papers, Archives of American Art, Smithsonian Institution, Washington, D.C. (hereafter AAA), microfilm roll 2076: frames 474, 495–6; and Marya Mannes, "Art on TV," *Art in America* 53, no. 6 (December–January 1965–6), p. 59. According to *TV Guide*, ("New Approach to the Old

Masters," p. 16), O'Doherty himself was guilty of sexual bias: "Discussing Da Vinci's 'Mona Lisa,' O'Doherty may remark: 'Women's smiles are ambivalent. Women don't know what they want. Men must make up their minds for them.'"

8 "Aline in Wonderland," Saarinen Papers, AAA, 2076: 495.

9 Shanley, "Art Class At Dawn."

10 See *Statistical Abstract of the United States 1960. 81st Annual Edition*, ed. Edwin D. Goldfield (Washington, D.C.: U.S. Government Printing Office, 1960), p. 520; *Statistical Abstract of the United States 1961. 82d Annual Edition*, ed. Edwin D. Goldfield (Washington, D.C.: U.S. Government Printing Office, 1961), p. 516; and *Statistical Abstract of the United States 1966. 87th Annual Edition*, ed. Edwin D. Goldfield (Washington, D.C.: U.S. Government Printing Office, 1966), p. 521. To compare 1965 U.S. statistics with those worldwide, see "Global viewing," *Time*, July 30, 1965, p. 64.

11 "Renaissance by Telecast," *Time*, October 16, 1939, p. 66; and Alton Kastner, "Television—For Art What Radio Was for Music," *Art Digest* 14, no. 6 (December 15, 1939), p. 22. See also Alton Kastner, "Television, Artist, and Public," *Magazine of Art* 33, no. 10 (October 1940), p. 581, where James Rowland Angell is quoted as saying "Television [will do] for art what radio has done for music." Sheeler's television appearances were broadcast on New York's NBC station W2XBS on October 6 and 11, 1939, the former (Friday) during the 2:30–3:30 p.m. slot, the latter (Wednesday) in the 8:30–9:30 p.m. slot. Although a typed script by Sheeler's dealer, Edith Halpert, titled "NBC TELEVISION (Time Capsule) / October 6, 1939," exists among her gallery's papers (Downtown Gallery Papers, AAA, 1883: 429), I have not yet located any mention of her in any published television listings; however, the script itself might have been used as an introduction to Sheeler's works on one of the broadcasts.

12 As proposed by Kastner, "Television—For Art What Radio Was for Music," pp. 22, 31; and Angell, cited above, no. 11. This viewpoint, however, was as much an assumption about television programming as it was about television viewership.

13 O'Doherty, "Art on Television," p. 114.

14 "All for Art," *Time*, July 20, 1959, p. 70.

15 *Advertising Age* (April 4, 1963), The Museum of Modern Art Papers, AAA, 5083: 44. See also the other magazine and newspaper clippings on this same microfilm roll, among them "about new york," *Cue* (January 26, 1963), on frame 12.

16 "The Artful Pitchman," *Newsweek*, April 26, 1965, p. 93, which refers to these commercials as "stunning showcase[s] of advanced photography, editing, direction, writing, music, and sound, all squeezed with ruthless discipline into a one-minute format"; and "They're Doing Something Right," *Time*, November 12, 1965, p. 95. On the advertising industry's awards handed out since 1960, see "Clio, Muse of History," *Time*, May 31, 1963, pp. 47–8.

17 "The Artful Pitchman."

18 In 1939, in alliance with NBC, MoMA became one of the first art institutions to sponsor and originate television art programs. Despite the brief broadcast times of that year—usually two hours per day, one hour slotted in mid-afternoon and another in early evening—and the paucity of available TV sets (1,000 to 2,000, according to one account), the museum nonetheless plunged into promoting both its personnel and the artists whose works it exhibited. Among the programs that aired during the summer and fall of 1939 were a show about the opening of its new building with its director, Alfred H. Barr, Jr., and trustee, Nelson Rockefeller, discussing Constantin Brancusi's *Bird in Space*; three lectures by the museum's director of education, Victor D'Amico; and the interviews with Charles Sheeler. On these early programs, see "Renaissance by Telecast"; Kastner, "Television—For

Art What Radio Was for Music" (which mentions the number of TV sets in the New York metropolitan area); and Kastner, "Television, Artist, and Public." MoMA continually promoted itself on television in future decades. For instance, "What Is Modern Art?" (1948), produced by the Princeton Film Center and filmed at the museum; *Dimension*'s "25th Anniversary of the Museum of Modern Art" (CBS; 1954); *Camera Three*'s "The Scope of Picasso" (CBS; 1957), made in conjunction with the museum's traveling exhibition *Picasso: Seventy-Fifth Anniversary*; *Wide Wide World*'s "A Star's Story" (NBC; 1958), which included a tour of the museum by film actress Joanne Woodward; and *Sunday*'s telecast (NBC; 1964) focusing on the museum's reopening, which included taped interviews by Saarinen with Alexander Calder, Marc Chagall, Stuart Davis, Alberto Giacometti, Joan Miró, and Henry Moore, along with pre-recorded studio visits with Henri Matisse and Constantin Brancusi.

19 For Seldes's remarks, see his essay, "Past and Present," *Television U.S.A.: 13 Seasons* (New York: The Museum of Modern Art, 1963), pp. 10–11.

20 Val Adams, "News of TV and Radio: Increasing Sponsor Interest in Public Affairs Programs Noted—Items," *New York Times*, January 24, 1960, sec. 2, p. 15. See also "A Need for Reform," *Time*, January 11, 1960, pp. 36–7.

21 Minow, appointed FCC chairman by Kennedy on January 10, 1961, resigned after just two and a half years in May 1963. In a speech delivered to the 39th Annual Convention of the National Association of Broadcasters in Washington, D.C., on May 9, 1961, he labeled television programming "a vast wasteland." For the entire text, see his *Equal Time: The Private Broadcaster and The Public Interest*, ed. Lawrence Laurent (New York: Atheneum, 1964), pp. 48–64.

22 Richard F. Shepard, "News Of TV And Radio: Networks Look for Advertiser Support for Public Affairs Shows—Notes," *New York Times*, January 3, 1960, sec. 2, p. 13.

23 "Frank Views on Art," Saarinen Papers, AAA, 2076: 475.

24 James Thrall Soby, "Art on TV," *Saturday Review*, April 13, 1957, p. 30, was remarking on programs of the 1950s, such as *The $64,000 Question* and fictionalized dramas on art and artists (*One Coat of White* and *Reclining Figure*). Among other skits similar to Allen's "Shtick Museum" was *The Red Skelton Show*'s "Go, Van Gogh" (CBS; May 10, 1962).

25 This statement was made in a 1949 interview of the artist at the Art Institute of Chicago by newspaper, television, and museum personnel. See the "Appendix" to Naomi Sawelson-Gorse, "The Art Institute of Chicago and the Arensberg Collection," *Art Institute of Chicago Museum Studies* 19, no. 1 (1993), p. 97.

26 Saarinen mentions the difference in attendance in "Frank Views On Art," Saarinen Papers, AAA, 2076: 475. Also in this year, television had replaced newspapers as the primary news source.

27 For example, on November 17, 1963, the communications satellite *Relay* enabled a live link between the National Gallery of Art in Washington, D.C., and the Louvre for an NBC special, "Museum without Walls," during which President Kennedy unveiled the *Mona Lisa*, then on loan. See Jack Gould, "TV: Museums via Relay," *New York Times*, November 18, 1963, p. 67; and Minow, *Equal Time*, p. 269.

28 Kennedy's press conference was to initiate the broadcast from the United States, but because it was delayed, a baseball game was shown instead.

29 For this characterization of women, see Diana M. Meehan, *Ladies of the Evening: Women Characters in Prime-Time Television* (Metuchen, N.J.: Scarecrow Press, 1983); and Spigel, "High Art in Low Places."

30 "A Tour of the White House with Mrs. John F. Kennedy" (CBS), first aired on a Wednesday evening (February 14, 1962), from 10:00 to 11:00 p.m. (Eastern); it was repeated during the daytime so that "school children" could watch the program on March 25, 1962, and January 13, 1963. Reportedly as many as 46,500,000 viewers saw the program, and "fourteen nations asked CBS for prints." For her

efforts in using television to bring the White House to the public, Jacqueline Kennedy received a Trustees Award from the Television Academy of Arts and Sciences in 1963.

31 This statement was made in opening remarks during a 1962 press conference in which Kennedy announced the Louvre's loan of the work.

32 *Accent*'s "Accent on 1961: A Public Memoir" (CBS) was telecast on January 4, 1962. As one media critic would later explain the phenomenon, Jacqueline Kennedy was "a mother—indeed, the national symbol of motherhood—and . . . a modern woman; a patron of the arts, a historical preservationist, and a key figure in producing the nation's collective memory": Michael Curtin, *Redeeming the Wasteland: Television Documentary and Cold War Politics* (New Brunswick, N.J.: Rutgers University Press, 1995), p. 241.

33 On *The Nation's Future* telecast with Hess and Canaday, see Jack Gould, "TV: Abstract Expressionism Debated," *New York Times*, June 4, 1962, p. 59. *Eyewitness*'s "The Art Show That Shocked America" was part live and part pre-recorded film. The program began and ended with narrator Collingwood crushed by throngs while attending the opening of the Armory Show's fiftieth-anniversary exhibition in New York, and was interspersed with pre-recorded film segments of his dialogues with Clark and Duchamp. *David Brinkley's Journal* would later highlight Jean Tinguely in a telecast named "The End of the World" (April 4, 1962).

34 Saarinen quoted in "Frank Views On Art," Saarinen Papers, AAA, 2076: 475; and August Heckscher, "The Arts and the National Government: Report to the President," Senate Document No. 28, 88th Congress, 1st Session (Washington, D.C.: U.S. Government Printing Office, 1963), p. vii, quoted in Don Adams and Arlene Goldbard, *Cultural Policy in U.S. History* (1986; 1995): www.wwcd.org/policy/US/Ushistory.html. Heckscher made similar comments on *Dorothy Gordon's Youth Forum*'s "What in Art Will Survive?" (NBC; June 3, 1963).

35 Jack Gould, "Television: A Wild Time in Store for Prime Time," *New York Times*, January 11, 1965, p. 125. On television viewing habits, see Gary A. Steiner, *The People Look at Television: A Study of Audience Attitudes: A Report of a Study at the Bureau of Applied Social Research, Columbia University* (New York: Knopf, 1963). See also the review of Steiner's book, "The Mass Tasteland," *Time*, March 1, 1963, p. 47.

36 "New Wing for 'Modern Art,'" *CBS Morning News*, May 26, 1964, Congressional Record Clippings, The Museum of Modern Art Papers, AAA, 5085: 396.

37 "Mrs. Johson [sic] re-dedicates N.Y. 'Modern Art,'" *Newsday*, May 26, 1964, Congressional Record Clippings, The Museum of Modern Art Papers, AAA, 5085: 393.

38 "A Visit to Washington with Mrs. Lyndon B. Johnson" (ABC color telecast; November 25, 1965).

39 Ada Louise Huxtable, "Federal States of Flux," *New York Times*, January 19, 1964, sec. 2, p. 22.

40 Mannes, "Art on TV." NET's color telecast profiles of Andy Warhol and Roy Lichtenstein in the series *USA: Artists* aired on March 8, 1966. Streisand's "Color Me Barbra" (CBS color telecast; March 30, 1966) included an eight-minute segment of her romping through the museum, sometimes in period costumes to match artworks on display (Streisand's first television special had her romping through Bergdorf Goodman, an upscale New York department store). "Gene Kelly in New York, New York," also a CBS color telecast, aired on February 14, 1966.

41 "TV's First War," *Newsweek*, August 30, 1965, p. 32. For example, Saarinen would interview wives of Army personnel serving in Vietnam for NBC's *Frank McGee Reports* (May 8, 1966); though she would continue covering art issues for the network, such as narrating "The Art Game," a one-shot program on the art market that likened it to a high-stakes football game (June 14, 1968; Saarinen Papers, AAA, 2076: 174–80), and reporting on the architecture of Miami, the site of the Republican Party's 1968 convention (August 4, 1968), among other topics.

Artists' Biographies and Bibliographies

COMPILED BY ERICA SHAMALY

Wallace Berman

Born 1926, Staten Island, New York
Died 1976, Topanga Canyon, California
Lived and worked in Topanga Canyon, California

Wallace Berman emerged as an artist in the late 1940s and was an originator of the West Coast assemblage movement of the 1960s. Berman's work drew upon the counterculture of 1950s and 1960s California, utilizing a montage of images and words from Beat and original poetry, Jewish mysticism, astrology, palmistry, jazz and blues, and the French Symbolist and Surrealist traditions. Throughout his career, Berman's oeuvre was deeply spiritual and personal in nature and consisted of works including large found-object sculptures, ink drawings of Hebrew letters on wood-stained paper, and collages made with the Verifax, an early form of copying machine. These works reveal his lifelong interest in the tension between the handmade and the mechanical, image and word, spirituality and materialism, and art and life, as these positions were played out in the panorama of postwar American culture. Characteristically unobtrusive in nature, Berman personally printed albums of poetry, photographs, and drawings for friends rather than showing works in galleries.

Art in Los Angeles: Seventeen Artists in the Sixties. Los Angeles: Los Angeles County Museum of Art, 1981.

Stich, Sidra. *Made in U.S.A.: An Americanization in Modern Art in the '50s & '60s*. Berkeley, California: University Art Museum, University of California, Berkeley, 1987.

Wallace Berman: Retrospective. Los Angeles: Fellows of Contemporary Art in cooperation with the Otis Art Institute Gallery, 1978.

Wallace Berman: Support the Revolution. Amsterdam, Holland: Institute of Contemporary Art, 1992.

Bruce Conner

Born 1933, McPherson, Kansas
Lives and works in San Francisco

Bruce Conner became known for his assemblages and films in the 1950s and 1960s. His moody found-object sculptures often combined women's nylon stockings, costume jewelry, bicycle wheels, and broken dolls with collaged or painted surfaces to create narrative works commenting on social mores and deviancies and personal visions of evolving spirituality. His short films of the same period—fast-paced montages deftly edited from found and new footage—challenged viewers to reevaluate the film-viewing experience. Connor's films forced viewers to assimilate copious narrative details and charged imagery within short periods of time, transforming perceptions of the work with each new viewing. Since the mid-1960s, his paintings, etchings, drawings, and woodcarvings have focused more on explaining the relationships among visual forms, while his films have evolved into more reflective works created with less chaotic technical methodology.

Boswell, Peter, Bruce Jenkins, and Joan Rothfuss. *2000 BC: The Bruce Conner Story Part II*. Minneapolis: Walker Art Center, 1999.

Bruce Conner: Assemblages, Paintings, Drawings, Engraving Collages 1960–1990. Santa Monica, California: Michael Kohn Gallery, 1990. Interview by Robert Dean and text by Dennis Hopper.

Bruce Conner: Sculpture, Assemblages, Collages, Drawings, Films. Philadelphia: Institute of Contemporary Art, University of Pennsylvania, 1967. Text by Joan C. Siegfried.

Lee Friedlander

Born 1934, Aberdeen, Washington
Lives and works in New York City

Lee Friedlander surfaced as an important interpreter of contemporary American life in the 1960s. Often described as a photographer of the social landscape, he is a master of the seemingly artless photograph of the street. Friedlander's work embodies an ostensibly effortless snapshot aesthetic that in actuality is dependent on a sophisticated technique challenging prescribed conventions of the photographic medium. His enigmatic images portray ambiguous situations and oddly appealing, idiosyncratic circumstances that distill character, time, and place. In these works, Friedlander reveals a real-life world of chaos and order and forthright emotion and alienation. His images of television screens in motel rooms he rented while on the road in the 1960s exemplify this aesthetic.

Like a One-Eyed Cat: Photographs by Lee Friedlander, 1956–1987. New York: Harry N. Abrams in association with the Seattle Art Museum, 1989. Text by Rod Slemmons.

K. O. Götz

Born 1914, Aachen, Germany
Lives and works in Niederbreitbach-Wolfenacker, Germany

Although Karl Otto Götz is perhaps best known for his expressionistic paintings, he also produced a less recognized, but pioneering, body of work exploring the relationships between art and technology: his *Rasterbilder* (Raster Pictures) of the 1950s and 1960s. While serving in a radar installation in Germany during World War II, Götz became intrigued by the images he saw on radar screens and was inspired to consider the potential of electronic technology as an art medium. After the war, Götz produced images using oscilloscopes and based on his study of information theory. These experiments eventually evolved into a new medium he called "electronic painting," which utilized imagery created from the transformation of information into electronic code. He produced his first *Rasterbilder* in 1959 and his first *Rasterfilms* a few years later.

Götz, Karl Otto. *Erinnerungen*. Aachen: Rimbaud, 1993–99.

Götz, Karl Otto. *K. O. Götz: Erinnerungen und Werk*. Dusseldorf: Concept Verlag, 1983.

Götz, Karl Otto. *K. O. Götz: Malerei, 1935–1993*. Dresden: Staatliche Kunstsammlungen Dresden, 1994.

Dennis Hopper

Born 1936, Dodge City, Kansas
Lives and works in Los Angeles

Actor, director, and artist Dennis Hopper practiced photography from 1954 to 1967, between the ages of eighteen and thirty-one. Hopper's black-and-white photographs capture the vitality and turbulence of American life in the 1960s by focusing on the people and places that were part of his daily life in California at the time, including some of the most prominent artists of the period. His rarely exhibited series of photographs of a television set broadcasting the funeral of President John F. Kennedy are among his most moving works. Hopper has appeared in such films as *Rebel without a Cause*, *True Grit*, and *Blue Velvet* and directed and starred in *Easy Rider*, among others. In the 1990s, he returned to the exploration of photography.

Hoberman, Jim. *Dennis Hopper: From Method to Madness*. Minneapolis: Walker Art Center, 1987.

Hopper, Dennis. *Out of the Sixties*. Pasadena, California: Twelvetrees Press, 1986.

Rodriguez, Elena. *Dennis Hopper: A Madness to His Method*. New York: St. Martin's Press, 1988.

Rolf Jährling

Born 1913, Dresden
Died 1991, Weidinger/Eifel, Germany

Rolf Jährling was an architect who founded the Galerie Parnass in Wuppertal, West Germany, in 1949 and served as its director until it closed in 1965. At the gallery, he presented more than 160 exhibitions and performances of the work of contemporary European and Asian artists, many of whom were associated with the *art informel* movement in France. In the early 1960s, Jährling began showing work by artists associated with Fluxus, including Nam June Paik's *Exposition of Music Electronic Television*. The most important of these projects was the concert *Kleines Sommerfest: Après John Cage* (Little Summer Festival: After John Cage) in 1962, which the artist and curator Jon Hendricks considers to be the first Fluxus performance. The last major Happening presented at Galerie Parnass before its closing was *24 Stunden* (24 Hours), which included performances by Joseph Beuys, Bazon Brock, Charlotte Moorman, Nam June Paik, Tomas Schmit, and Wolf Vostell.

Baltzer, Will and Alfons W. Biermann, eds. *Treffpunkt Parnass Wuppertal 1949–1965*. Cologne and Bonn: Rheinland-Verlag, 1980.

Ray Johnson

Born 1927, Detroit, Michigan
Died 1995, Sag Harbor, New York
Lived and worked in Locust Valley, New York

Ray Johnson's unclassifiable output is considered an important antecedent to Pop Art, performance art, and Fluxus. Johnson began his career as an Abstract Expressionist painter, but he ultimately refocused his talents after moving to New York City in 1948 and developing friendships with such artists as Robert Rauschenberg and Cy Twombly. In the mid-1950s, he began working with small collages he labeled "moticos," combinations of erratically shaped ink drawings, newspaper clippings, and portraits of celebrities. Johnson first showed them on the street or in other public places, and these unconventional presentations are considered precursors of the earliest Happenings. Johnson's most notable and long-lasting contribution was the creation of the New York Correspondence School, an international collaboration of artists and poets in the early 1960s who utilized the postal service to exchange artworks, objects, and anything else considered significant by participants. Johnson's original impetus continues to spawn generations of mail artists after thirty years, with involvement from dozens of countries.

De Salvo, Donna and Catherine Gudis, eds. *Ray Johnson: Correspondences*. Columbus, Ohio: Wexner Center for the Arts, 1999.

Ray Johnson. Philadelphia: The Galleries at Moore, 1991. Foreword by Elsa Longhauser.

Edward Kienholz

Born 1927, Fairfield, Washington
Died 1994, Hope, Idaho
Lived and worked in Hope, Idaho; Houston, Texas; and Berlin

With the assemblages, installations, and tableaux that Edward Kienholz began to produce in the late 1950s, and later environments created since 1972 with his wife, Nancy Reddin Kienholz, he exposed the hypocrisy and cruelty embedded in American consumer culture. After he emerged as an artist in the context of the Beat movement on the West Coast during the 1950s, his work evolved during the 1960s out of an idealist reaction against the political and social turmoil of the decade. Kienholz is perhaps best known for his sculptures and stage-like environments of this period that were constructed with found objects from everyday life—ranging from televisions to pieces of furniture or automobiles—which addressed the human alienation within contemporary society.

Kienholz, Edward, Nancy Reddin Kienholz, and Walter Hopps. *Kienholz: A Retrospective*. New York: Whitney Museum of American Art, 1996.

Manfred Leve

Born 1936, Trier, Germany
Lives and works in Nuremberg

Manfred Leve has photographed artists ranging from John Cage to Gerhard Richter for more than forty years, creating an invaluable record of the history of art in the second half of the twentieth century. He documented many of the Fluxus exhibitions, performances, events, and actions that occurred in Europe during the late 1950s and 1960s. In 1963, he extensively photographed Nam June Paik's ten-day exhibition *Exposition of Music Electronic Television* at Galerie Parnass in Wuppertal, Germany. His photographs of this ephemeral Fluxus installation document one of the first incarnations of television in art, consisting of Paik's altered television sets and "electronic paintings," and the involvement of visitors and participants, including such artists as Wolf Vostell, Joseph Beuys, and K. O. Götz. Leve continues to travel the world to photograph artists.

Aktionen, Vernissagen, Personen: Die Rheinische Kunstszene der 50er und 60er Jahre. Eine Fotodokumentation von Manfred Leve. Cologne: Rheinland-Verlag and Nuremberg: Institut für moderne Kunst Nürnberg, 1982.

Block, Rene. *Eine lange Geschichte mit vielen Knoten: Fluxus in Deutschland, 1962–1994.* Stuttgart: Institut für Auslandsbeziehungen, 1995.

George Maciunas

Born 1931, Kaunus, Lithuania
Died 1978, Boston
Lived and worked in New York City

An avid scholar of art, art history, graphics, architecture, and musicology, George Maciunas established and propelled the Fluxus movement of the 1960s after participating in music composition classes at the New School for Social Research in New York (along with such artists as George Brecht and Dick Higgins). Fluxus is an alternative interdisciplinary movement liberating artists from established art traditions by promoting "anti-art," and is connected to Dada, performance art and Happenings, installation art, and conceptualism. From 1961 until his death in 1978, Maciunas organized cooperative Fluxus activities and musical and literary events featuring like-minded avant-garde artists. He also designed *AN ANTHOLOGY*, a collection of works that developed into the prototype for the graphic style that later characterized Fluxus.

Hendricks, Jon. *Fluxus Codex.* Detroit: The Gilbert and Lila Silverman Fluxus Collection in association with Harry N. Abrams, New York, 1988.

Williams, Emmett, Ann Noël, and Ay-O. *Mr. Fluxus: A Collective Portrait of George Maciunas, 1931–1978.* London: Thames and Hudson, 1997.

Peter Moore

Born 1932, London
Died 1993, New York City
Lived and worked in New York City

Peter Moore's photographs of the New York art world in the 1960s and 1970s are among the most complete and captivating documents of this intensely active era. In addition to photographing such artists as Nam June Paik and Wolf Vostell, Moore photographed performances, actions, Happenings, dance, and other transitory events that survive now only through his documentation.

Hendricks, Jon. *Fluxus Codex.* Detroit: The Gilbert and Lila Silverman Fluxus Collection in association with Harry N. Abrams, New York, 1988.

Ugo Mulas

Born 1928, Pozzolengo, Italy
Died 1972, Milan, Italy
Lived and worked in Milan, Italy

Ugo Mulas was a photographer who documented the art scene in Europe and the United States, among other subjects. After being introduced to Pop Art in 1964, Mulas traveled to New York City to document such artists as Robert Rauschenberg, as he considered Pop Art a seminal movement that liberated artists from the constraints of art traditions. He produced an essential corpus of images that was published in the book *New York: The New Art Scene* in 1967. This publication offers a rare glimpse of artists working and engaging in the activities of everyday life at home in their studios.

Mulas, Ugo. *New York: The New Art Scene*. New York: Holt, Rinehart and Winston, 1967. Text by Alan Solomon.

Ugo Mulas, fotografo 1928–1973. Geneva: Musée d'art et d'histoire, 1984.

Yoko Ono

Born 1933, Tokyo
Lives and works in New York City

Yoko Ono is an artist, composer, and activist who played a leading role in the avant-garde art scene that coalesced in New York City in the 1960s. After World War II, Ono and her family left Japan to join relatives in the United States, and in 1956 she moved to New York City to pursue her artistic career. In addition to sponsoring a series of legendary art and music performances at her Chambers Street loft, Ono began to produce a body of work in the context of the burgeoning movement known as Fluxus. These works, which often took the form of scores, reflected her interest in simplified and repetitive formal structures, utilizing common objects from everyday life, and timely social and political issues. In 1964, Ono published the first edition of her book *Grapefruit*, featuring sections on music, painting, events, poetry, objects, film, and dance.

Hendricks, Jon, ed. *Yoko Ono: To See the Skies*. Milan: Mazzotta, 1990.

Ono, Yoko. *Grapefruit: Works and Drawings by Yoko Ono*. New York: Simon and Schuster, 1970.

Yoko Ono: Have You Seen the Horizon Lately? Oxford: Museum of Modern Art, 1997.

Nam June Paik

Born 1932, Seoul, Korea
Lives and works in New York City

Nam June Paik is perhaps the most influential video artist of his generation. He played a pioneering role in the evolution of video as an art form and, since the 1950s, has continued to expand the frontiers of the medium. While living in Germany in 1963, Paik became one of the first artists to use working television sets by distorting their reception of broadcast transmissions and creating interactive video works that transformed the viewer's relationship to the medium. In 1964 he moved to New York, where he continued his explorations of video; by the end of the decade, he had become one of the leading figures in a new generation of artists creating an aesthetic discourse out of television and the moving image.

Decker, Edith. *Paik Video*. Cologne: DuMont Buchverlag, 1988.

Hanhardt, John G. *The Worlds of Nam June Paik*. New York: Solomon R. Guggenheim Museum, 2000.

Herzogenrath, Wulf. *Nam June Paik, Werke 1946–1976: Musik—Fluxus—Video*. Cologne: Kölnischer Kunstverein, 1976.

Paik, Nam June. *Nam June Paik: Avante Garde Video*. [Film] San Francisco: 1987.

Paik, Nam June. *Nam June Paik: Video Time, Video Space*. New York: Harry N. Abrams, 1993.

Robert Rauschenberg

Born 1925, Port Arthur, Texas
Lives and works in Captiva, Florida

An artistic chameleon, Robert Rauschenberg embraces painting, sculpture, printmaking, photography, performance, dance, technology, and the spaces between these mediums. A native of Texas, Rauschenberg moved to New York in the 1940s and immediately began to imbue the formal languages of European modernist art with a distinctly American vernacular. In the mid-1950s, he began to produce his first "Combines," works that synthesized the gestural brushwork of Abstract Expressionism with objects and images from everyday life. For only two years, beginning in 1962, Rauschenberg used commercially prepared silkscreens for transferring a cacophony of images from magazines, newspapers, and original photographs onto canvas, which he then combined with additional painterly passages. After winning first prize for painting at the 1964 Venice Biennale, Rauschenberg had a friend destroy the screens used to create the silkscreen paintings, thereby guaranteeing his transition to something entirely fresh. In the 1960s he began an ongoing collaboration with engineer Billy Klüver to produce a series of sculptures and installations incorporating technology.

Feinstein, Roni. *Robert Rauschenberg: The Silkscreen Paintings, 1962–64*. New York: Whitney Museum of American Art, 1990.

Hopps, Walter, and Susan Davidson. *Robert Rauschenberg: A Retrospective*. New York: Solomon R. Guggenheim Foundation, 1997.

James Rosenquist

Born 1933, Grand Forks, North Dakota
Lives and works in Aripeka, Florida, and New York City

James Rosenquist is a painter and printmaker who established himself as a leading Pop artist in the early 1960s after experimenting with Abstract Expressionism in the late 1950s. As he was trained as a billboard artist in Minnesota and New York, his work from the early 1960s onward implements imagery and techniques used in billboard advertising, which led to his classification as a Pop artist. Unlike fellow Pop artists Robert Indiana, Robert Rauschenberg, and Andy Warhol, Rosenquist went further than simply elevating advertising and popular culture images to "fine art" status. Instead, he created large-scale paintings utilizing montages of seemingly unrelated popular images that were amalgamated into seamless fields, imbuing his works with mysteriously surrealist qualities.

Castelli, Leo. *James Rosenquist: The Big Paintings: Thirty Years*. New York: 1994.

Goldman, Judith. *James Rosenquist*. New York: 1985.

Goldman, Judith. *James Rosenquist: The Early Pictures, 1961–1964*. New York: Gagosian Gallery, 1992.

Wolf Vostell

Born 1932, Leverkusen, Germany
Died 1998, Berlin
Lived and worked in Berlin

One of the best-known artists of the Fluxus and Happenings movements in the 1960s, Wolf Vostell was a prolific creator of paintings, assemblages, installations, drawings, photography, films, and performances. He was one of the first artists to repeatedly integrate television sets and video imagery into his installations. In many of his works, he appropriated imagery from American and European consumer culture and objects from everyday life. Vostell imaginatively transformed these images and objects into the essential components of works that critiqued the physical, psychological, and social violence seemingly endemic in postwar American and European society.

Vostell, Wolf. *dé-coll/age happenings*. Translated by Laura P. Williams. New York: Something Else Press, 1966.

Vostell: Retrospective, 1958–1974. Berlin: Neuer Berliner Kunstverein, 1975.

Wedewer, Rolf, ed. *Vostell*. Heidelberg: Edition Braus, 1992.

Andy Warhol

Born 1928, Pittsburgh
Died 1987, New York City
Lived and worked in New York City

Although he achieved success as a commercial artist in New York in the 1950s, Andy Warhol rose to prominence in the art world with his silkscreen paintings of the 1960s. He utilized iconic images such as Campbell's Soup cans, dollar bills, Coca-Cola bottles, and faces of celebrities to comment on the predictability, harshness, and ambiguity of American society. His infatuation with celebrity, death, and the carnival of American popular culture converged in the films that he began producing during that decade. He shot most of these films at "The Factory," the name of his studio in New York, where he gathered a circle of friends and collaborators he referred to as his "Superstars."

Andy Warhol: Death and Disasters. Houston: The Menil Collection and Houston Fine Art Press, 1988.

Bourdon, David. *Warhol*. New York: Harry N. Abrams, 1989.

McShine, Kynaston. *Andy Warhol: A Retrospective*. New York: The Museum of Modern Art, 1989.

Warhol, Andy. *The Philosophy of Andy Warhol from A to B (and Back Again)*. New York: Harcourt Brace Jovanovich, 1975.

Warhol, Andy, and Pat Hackett. *POPism: The Warhol '60s*. New York: Harcourt Brace Jovanovich, 1980.

Tom Wesselmann

Born 1931, Cincinnati
Lives and works in New York City

Tom Wesselmann gained prominence in the 1960s with his monumental paintings rendered in a style reminiscent of popular advertising, a direct result of the explosion of postwar consumer culture in the United States. In these works, he reinvigorated the traditional genres of figure and still-life painting by depicting scenes from daily life. The women in his figure paintings are more reminiscent of pin-up models than idealized female nudes from earlier art history, and instead of portraying fruits and flowers in his still lifes, he pictured brand-name products available at supermarkets; the tactile quality of these works suggests the smooth surfaces of products such as cars and refrigerators. In many of these works, Wesselmann incorporated actual photographs, advertisements, reproductions of artworks, and objects, including television sets—another means by which he attempted to bridge the gap between art and life.

Hunter, Sam. *Tom Wesselmann*. New York: Rizzoli, 1994.

Stealingworth, Slim. *Tom Wesselmann*. New York: Abbeville Press, 1980.

Tom Wesselmann. Early Still Lifes: 1962–1964. Balboa, California: Newport Harbor Art Museum, 1971.

Garry Winogrand

Born 1928, New York City
Died 1984, Tijuana, Mexico
Lived and worked in New York City; Austin, Texas; and Los Angeles

Garry Winogrand, one of the most influential American photographers of his generation, abandoned painting in the early 1950s to work as both a commercial and a fine art photographer. Influenced by the photographers Walker Evans and Robert Frank, he developed a distinctive snapshot aesthetic. Winogrand aimed for instinctive, narrative photographs that required little or no explanatory text. He is perhaps best known for his captivating images of urban life—street and nightlife scenes, zoos, awards ceremonies, and art gallery openings.

Szarkowski, John. *Winogrand: Figments from the Real World*. New York: The Museum of Modern Art, 1988.

Winogrand, Garry. *The Man in the Crowd: The Uneasy Streets of Garry Winogrand*. San Francisco: Fraenkel Gallery, 1998. Text by Ben Lifson.

Bibliography

Barnouw, Eric. *Tube of Plenty: The Evolution of American Television*. New York: Oxford University Press, 1975.

Baudrillard, Jean. *Simulations*. New York: Semiotext(e), 1983.

Boddy, William. *Fifties Television: The Industry and Its Critics*. Chicago: University of Illinois Press, 1990.

Debord, Guy. *The Society of the Spectacle*. Translated by Donald Nicholson-Smith. New York: Zone Books, 1994.

Fisher, David E., and Marshall Jon Fisher. *Tube: The Invention of Television*. Washington, D.C.: Counterpoint, 1996.

Geller, Matthew, ed. *From Receiver to Remote Control: The TV Set*. New York: New Museum of Contemporary Art, 1990.

Hall, Doug, and Sally Jo Fifer, eds. *Illuminating Video: An Essential Guide to Video Art*. New York: Aperture in association with the Bay Area Collective, 1990.

Hapgood, Susan. *Neo-Dada: Redefining Art, 1958–62*. New York: American Federation of Arts in association with Universe Publishing, 1994.

Heiferman, Marvin, and Lisa Phillips. *Image World: Art and Media Culture*. New York: Whitney Museum of American Art, 1989.

Kaplan, E. Ann. *Regarding Television: Critical Approaches—An Anthology*. Frederick, Maryland: University Publications of America in association with the American Film Institute, 1983.

Kellner, Douglas. *Jean Baudrillard: From Marxism to Postmodernism and Beyond*. Stanford: Stanford University Press, 1989.

Marling, Karal Ann. *As Seen on TV: The Visual Culture of Everyday Life in the 1950s*. Cambridge, Massachusetts: Harvard University Press, 1994.

McLuhan, Marshall. *Understanding Media: The Extensions of Man*. New York: McGraw-Hill, 1964.

Mellencamp, Patricia, ed. *Logics of Television: Essays in Cultural Criticism*. Bloomington: Indiana University Press, 1990.

Spigel, Lynn. *Make Room for TV: Television and the Family Ideal in Postwar America*. Chicago: University of Chicago Press, 1992.

Stich, Sidra. *Made in U.S.A.: An Americanization in Modern Art, the '50s and '60s*. Berkeley: University Art Museum, University of California, 1987.

Watson, Mary Ann. *The Expanding Vista: American Television in the Kennedy Years*. New York: Oxford University Press, 1990.

Williams, Raymond. *Television: Technology and Cultural Form*. New York: Schocken Books, 1974.

Zelizer, Barbie. *Covering the Body: The Kennedy Assassination, the Media, and the Shaping of Collective Memory*. Chicago: University of Chicago Press, 1992.

Exhibition Checklist

Height precedes width precedes depth. Photograph dimensions are paper size.

WALLACE BERMAN

Papa's got a brand new bag, 1964
Mixed media
42 × 30⅝ inches (107 × 78 cm)
Courtesy Nicole Klagsbrun Gallery, New York

Untitled, 1964
Verifax collage
7¼ × 9¾ inches (18 × 25 cm)
Collection of Dennis Hopper

BRUCE CONNER

REPORT. A Film by Bruce Conner, 1963–67
16mm film, black and white, 13 minutes
Print Courtesy of Bruce Conner and Canyon Cinema

LEE FRIEDLANDER

Philadelphia, 1961
Gelatin silver print
11 × 14 inches (28 × 36 cm)
Courtesy Fraenkel Gallery, San Francisco

Washington, D.C., 1962
Gelatin silver print
14 × 11 inches (36 × 28 cm)
Courtesy Fraenkel Gallery, San Francisco

Florida, 1963
Gelatin silver print
11 × 14 inches (28 × 36 cm)
Courtesy Fraenkel Gallery, San Francisco

New York State, 1965
Gelatin silver print
14 × 11 inches (36 × 28 cm)
Courtesy Fraenkel Gallery, San Francisco

K. O. GÖTZ

Density 10:3:2:1, 1960
Felt pen on cardboard on canvas
79 × 108 inches (200 × 260 cm)
Collection of the artist

Statistisch-metrische Modulation 12:2:1, 1960
Felt pen on cardboard
20 × 26 inches (50 × 65 cm)
Collection of the artist

Statistisch-metrische Modulation 12:3:1, 1960
Felt pen on cardboard
20 × 26 inches (50 × 65 cm)
Collection of the artist

DENNIS HOPPER

Kennedy Funeral, 1963
Suite of eight gelatin silver prints
16 × 24 inches (41 × 61 cm) each
Courtesy of the artist and Tony Shafrazi Gallery, New York

RAY JOHNSON

One TV, 1964
Ink and collage with Korean stamps
5⅜ × 3⅞ inches (14 × 10 cm)
Collection of William S. Wilson, New York

EDWARD KIENHOLZ

The Big Eye (Homage to H.S.), 1961
Painted television console, plastic, newspaper, and figurine
56 × 24 × 30 inches (142 × 61 × 76 cm)
Collection Onnasch, Berlin

PETER MOORE

Nam June Paik with original *Demagnetizer* (or *Life Ring*), New York, October 1965
Gelatin silver print
8 × 10 inches (20 × 25 cm)
Courtesy Estate of Peter Moore/ Bound & Unbound, New York

Nam June Paik with *Magnet TV*, New York, October 1965
Gelatin silver print
8 × 10 inches (20 × 25 cm)
Courtesy Estate of Peter Moore/ Bound & Unbound, New York

"Double-yoke experiments" from *Distorted TVs*, from the exhibition *Electronic Art*, Galería Bonino, New York, November 1965
Gelatin silver print
8 × 10 inches (20 × 25 cm)
Courtesy Estate of Peter Moore/ Bound & Unbound, New York

UGO MULAS

Untitled (Robert Rauschenberg working in his studio in New York City with portable television set on cart to the left), ca. 1964
Gelatin silver print
11 × 15 inches (28 × 39 cm)
Archivio Ugo Mulas, Milan

Untitled (Robert Rauschenberg in his studio in New York City with portable television set behind him), ca. 1964
11 × 15 inches (28 × 39 cm)
Archivio Ugo Mulas, Milan

Untitled (Robert Rauschenberg with Elaine Sturtevant in his studio in New York City, while Steve Paxton and Rauschenberg's son, Christopher, watch television), 1965
Gelatin silver print
11 × 15 inches (28 × 39 cm)
Archivio Ugo Mulas, Milan

Untitled (Lee Bontecou watching television in her studio in New York City), ca. 1965
Gelatin silver print
11 × 15 inches (28 × 39 cm)
Archivio Ugo Mulas, Milan

YOKO ONO

Sky TV, 1966
2000 realization for this exhibition
Security camera, cable, and vintage television
Dimensions variable
Collection of the artist

NAM JUNE PAIK

Zen for TV, 1963/2000
Prepared television set
Dimensions variable
Collection of the Austin Museum of Art

NAM JUNE PAIK DOCUMENTATION

Exposition of Music Electronic Television, Galerie Parnass, Wuppertal, Germany, March 1963:

Photographs by Rolf Jährling
Sixteen gelatin silver prints
8 × 10 inches (20 × 25 cm) or 10 × 8 inches (25 × 20 cm) each
The Gilbert and Lila Silverman Fluxus Collection, Detroit

Photographs by Manfred Leve
Two gelatin silver prints
9½ × 11⅞ inches (24 × 30 cm) each
Courtesy Galerie Berndt Kunsthandel GmbH, Cologne

Photographs by George Maciunas
Two gelatin silver prints
10 × 8 inches (25 × 20 cm) each
The Gilbert and Lila Silverman Fluxus Collection, Detroit

Exhibition poster from *Exposition of Music Electronic Television*, Galerie Parnass, Wuppertal, Germany, March 1963
Silkscreen on newspaper and offset on translucent paper with texts by Nam June Paik and Jean-Pierre Wilhelm
Each sheet, 10 × 14 inches (25 × 36 cm)
Collection of Jon and Joanne Hendricks, New York

Letter from George Maciunas to Robert Watts, March 11 or 12, 1963
Holograph black ink on yellow lined paper, one side
11 × 8 inches (28 × 20 cm)
The Gilbert and Lila Silverman Fluxus Collection, Detroit

fLuxus cc fiVe ThReE (Fluxus newspaper, no. 4, June 1964), featuring Nam June Paik's text "afterlude to the EXPOSITION of EXPERIMENTAL TELEVISION, 1963, March, Galerie Parnass"
Offset on paper
22¾ × 18 inches (58 × 46 cm)
The Gilbert and Lila Silverman Fluxus Collection, Detroit

ROBERT RAUSCHENBERG

Straw Boss, 1962
Oil and silkscreen on canvas
96 × 60 inches (244 × 152 cm)
Weatherspoon Art Gallery, The University of North Carolina at Greensboro, Charles and Laura Dwan Memorial Gift, 1982

Shades, 1964
Lithographic object consisting of six Plexiglas panels, aluminum frame, and light bulb
15 × 14 × 11¾ inches (38 × 36 × 30 cm)
Published by U.L.A.E. in an edition of 24, plus 3 A.P.
Art Collection, Harry Ransom Humanities Research Center, The University of Texas at Austin

JAMES ROSENQUIST

Aspen, Colorado, 1966
Oil on canvas
48 × 62 inches (122 × 57 cm)
Private Collection
Courtesy Sonnabend Gallery, New York

WOLF VOSTELL

TV-dé-coll/age, No. 1, 1958–59
Six television sets behind canvas
99 × 134 × 32 inches (250 × 340 × 80 cm)
Courtesy Fine Art Rafael Vostell, Berlin

TV für Millionen (TV for Millions), 1959/65
Tuned television set
19¾ × 22½ × 17¾ inches (50 × 57 × 45 cm)
Museum of Modern Art Ludwig Foundation Vienna, formerly Hahn Collection, Cologne

TV-dé-coll/age for millions, 1959
Offset poster from *dé-coll/age happenings* (New York: Something Else Press, 1966)
21⅝ × 16½ inches (55 × 42 cm)
The Museum of Modern Art Library, New York

Documentation of performance of *TV-dé-coll/age* action performed on George Segal's farm near South Brunswick, New Jersey, May 19, 1963
Photographs by Peter Moore
Five gelatin silver prints
8 × 10 inches (20 × 25 cm) or 10 × 8 inches (25 × 20 cm) each
Courtesy Estate of Peter Moore/ Bound & Unbound, New York

Documentation of exhibition *Wolf Vostell & TV-dé-coll/age & dé-coll/age Posters & Comestible dé-coll/age*, Smolin Gallery, New York, May 22–June 8, 1963
Photographs by Peter Moore
Two gelatin silver prints
10 × 8 inches (25 × 20 cm) each
Courtesy Estate of Peter Moore/ Bound & Unbound, New York

TV-dé-coll/age: & Morning Glory; 2 pieces, 1963
Artist's book (New York: Smolin Gallery, 1963)
6 × 4 × 2 inches (15 × 10 × 5 cm)
Rare Books and Manuscripts, The Ohio State University Libraries, Columbus

ANDY WARHOL

Jackie, 1964
(Eight paintings from the series)
Silkscreen ink on synthetic polymer paint on canvas
20 × 16 inches (50.8 × 40.6 cm) each
The Andy Warhol Museum, Pittsburgh
Founding Collection, Contribution The Andy Warhol Foundation for the Visual Arts, Inc.

Flash—November 22, 1963, 1968
Portfolio, with cover, consisting of eleven serigraphs, plus an additional suite of three
Cover: 22¼ × 21¾ inches (56.5 × 55.2 cm)
Each serigraph: 21 × 21 inches (53.3 × 53.3 cm)
The Menil Collection, Houston

Outer and Inner Space, 1965
16mm film, black and white, sound, transferred to video, 33 minutes, double screen
The Andy Warhol Museum, Pittsburgh

TOM WESSELMANN

Great American Nude #27, 1962
Enamel, casein, and collage
48 × 36 inches (122 × 91 cm)
The Mayor Gallery, London

Still Life #28, 1963
Acrylic, collage, and television set on board
48 × 60 inches (122 × 152 cm)
Collection of Robert E. Abrams

GARRY WINOGRAND

Democratic National Convention, Los Angeles, 1960
Gelatin silver print
20 × 16 inches (51× 41 cm)
Courtesy Fraenkel Gallery, San Francisco

MEDIA SECTION

A selection of commercials from the late 1950s to the late 1960s

The Abraham Zapruder Film, November 22, 1963
Color, 26 seconds
Collection of the Dallas County Historical Foundation, The Sixth Floor Museum at Dealey Plaza c/o Silverberg

The Four Dark Days: From Dallas to Arlington, Black-and-white television program, 2 hours 26 minutes, originally broadcast on CBS, November 25, 1963

PHOTOGRAPHY CREDITS

Photographs in this catalogue have been supplied, in the majority of cases, by the owners or custodians of the works, as cited in the captions. The following list applies to photographs for which an additional acknowledgment is due.

© 2000 Artists Rights Society (ARS), New York/ VG Bild-Kunst, Bonn: pp. 30, 50, 51

© Estate of Wallace Berman/LA Louver, Venice, California. Photo by Alan Shaffer, Venice, California: p. 38

© Estate of Wallace Berman/LA Louver, Venice, California: p. 39

CBS Photo Archive: pp. 19, 68, 78, 81

© Estate of Ray Johnson: p. 40

© Estate of Edward Kienholz, LA Louver, Venice, California. Photo by J. Littkemann, Berlin: p. 22

© Manfred Leve, Nuremberg: p. 47 (bottom right)

Courtesy Meadowlane Enterprises. Inc. Photo by 501 Post, Austin: p. 77

© Estate of Peter Moore/Licensed by VAGA, New York, NY: pp. 48, 52–53, 102–103

© Ugo Mulas Estate. All Rights Reserved: inside front cover, pp. 28–29

© James Rosenquist/Licensed by VAGA, New York, NY: pp. frontispiece, 34

Photo by Jeff Rowe, Austin Prints for Publication: pp. 45, back cover

Photo by Alan Shaffer, Venice, California: pp. 38, 56–57

© The Gilbert and Lila Silverman Fluxus Collection, Detroit: pp. 46, 47 (top and center left)

Photo by Oren Slor, New York: pp. 44, 70

© Untitled Press, Inc./Licensed by VAGA, New York, NY: pp. 36, 37

Courtesy Walker Art Center, Minneapolis. Photo by Dan Dennehy: pp. 60, 61, 62

© 2000 The Andy Warhol Museum, Pittsburgh, PA, a museum of Carnegie Institute: pp. 64–65, inside back cover

© 2000 Andy Warhol Foundation for the Visual Arts/Artists Rights Society (ARS), New York, Photo by Richard Stoner: p. 8, 63. Photo by Paul Hester, Houston: pp. 58–59

© Tom Wesselmann/Licensed by VAGA, New York, NY: p. 42. Photo by Jim Strong, New York: pp. 2–3, 41

© 1984 The Estate of Garry Winogrand. All Rights Reserved. Copyprint: © 2000 The Museum of Modern Art, New York: p. 16

This publication was typeset in Filosophia and Univers Extended using QuarkXPress on a Macintosh 9600 and printed on Warren Lustro Offset Enamel Dull by The Studley Press Inc., Dalton, Massachusetts.

Austin Museum of Art

STAFF

William J. O'Brien
President and Chief Executive Officer

Elizabeth Ferrer
The Dr. and Mrs. Ernest C. Butler
Executive Director

Debe Bentley
Cheryl Black
Michaela Black
Alicia Bowman
Andrea Casey
Melissa Cherry
Jessica Clendenon
Lisa Dirks
Kasey Eggleston
Julie Eskoff
Dana Friis-Hansen
Ben Fyffe
John Gamblin
Jeffrie Gioe
Sonia Gonzalez
Julia Hart
Mary Herr
Christi Hill
Molly Hipp
Joe Janson
Kelli Johnson
Philip Just
Valerie Kanak
Susan Kemner Reed
Kristin Kimbrell
Lisa Knab
Stacey Koenig
Melissa Lopez
Tim Lowke

Ari Luber
Enrique Martinez
Aaron Mendenhall
Julie Merry
April Meyers
Jill Morena
Dave Moreno
Heather Nash
Bill Nichols
Jean Page
Jennifer Peel
Marisa Pisano
David Reed
Shelly Reese
Kate Robertson
Todd Sandel
Gail Sanders
Erica Shamaly
Cecile Shopen
Judith Sims
April Stallman
James Tisdale
Frank Treviño
Mary Dalaina Trotter
Sharon Truman
Tony Truong
Cullen Turk

as of July 1, 2000

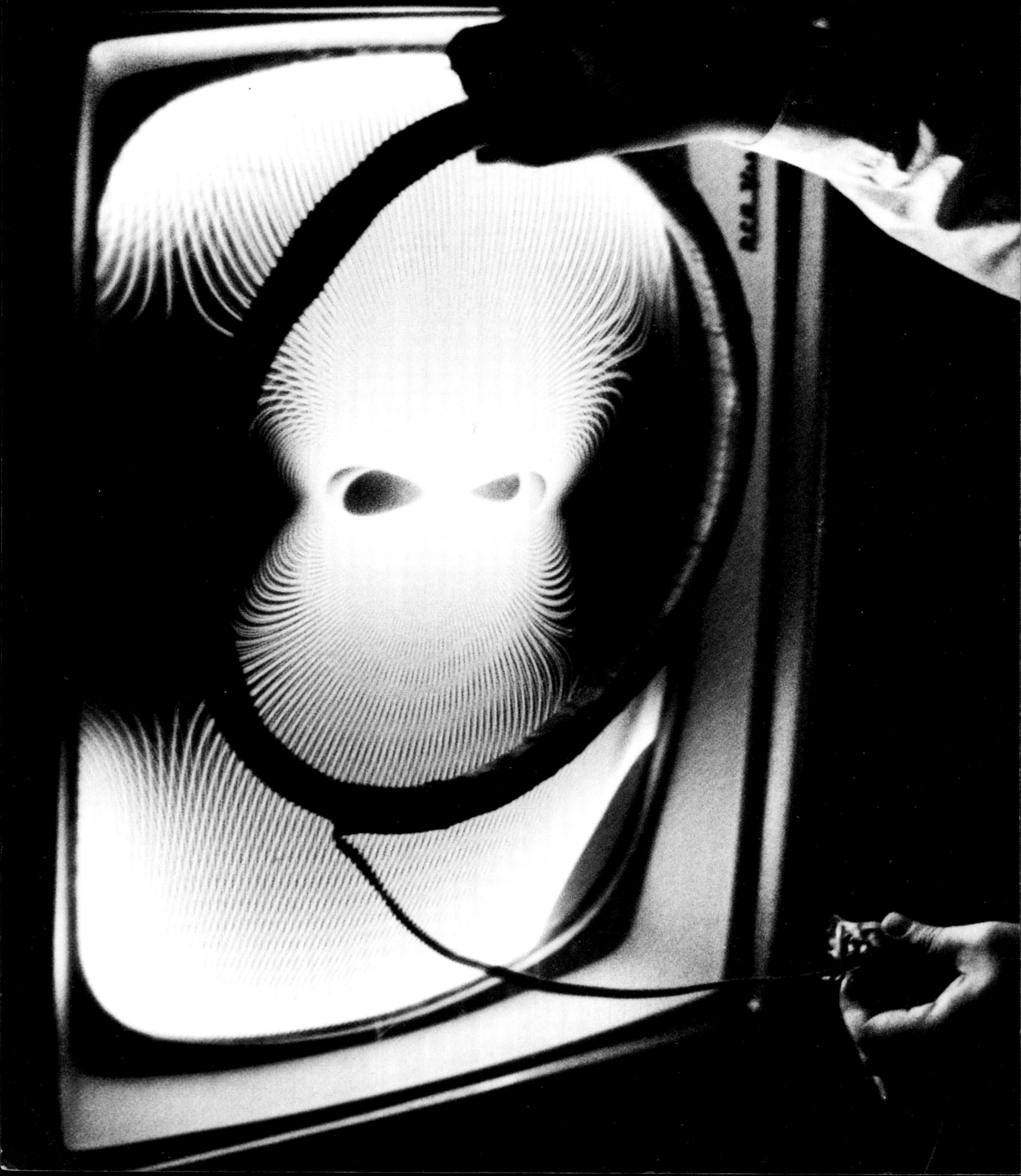

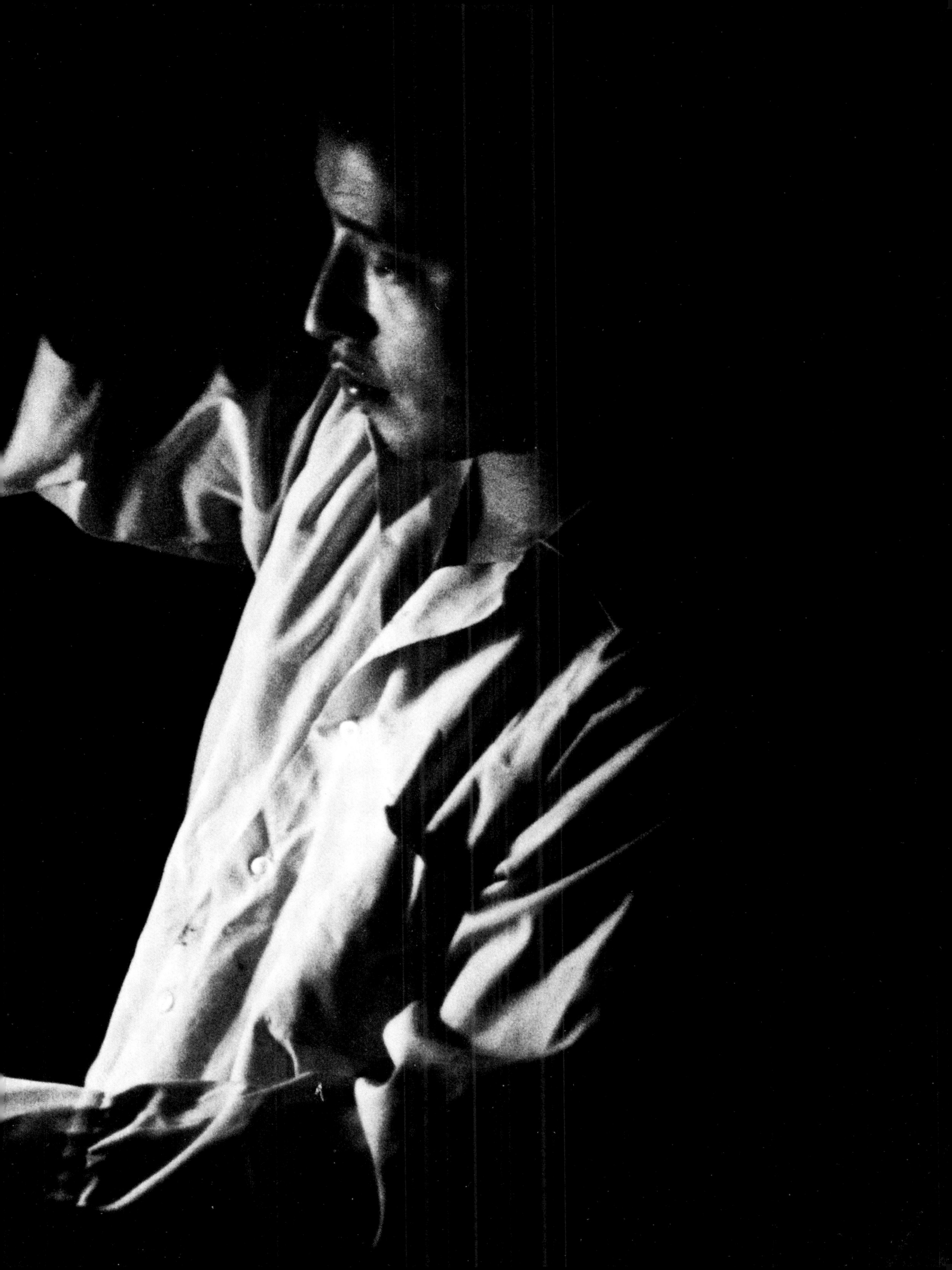

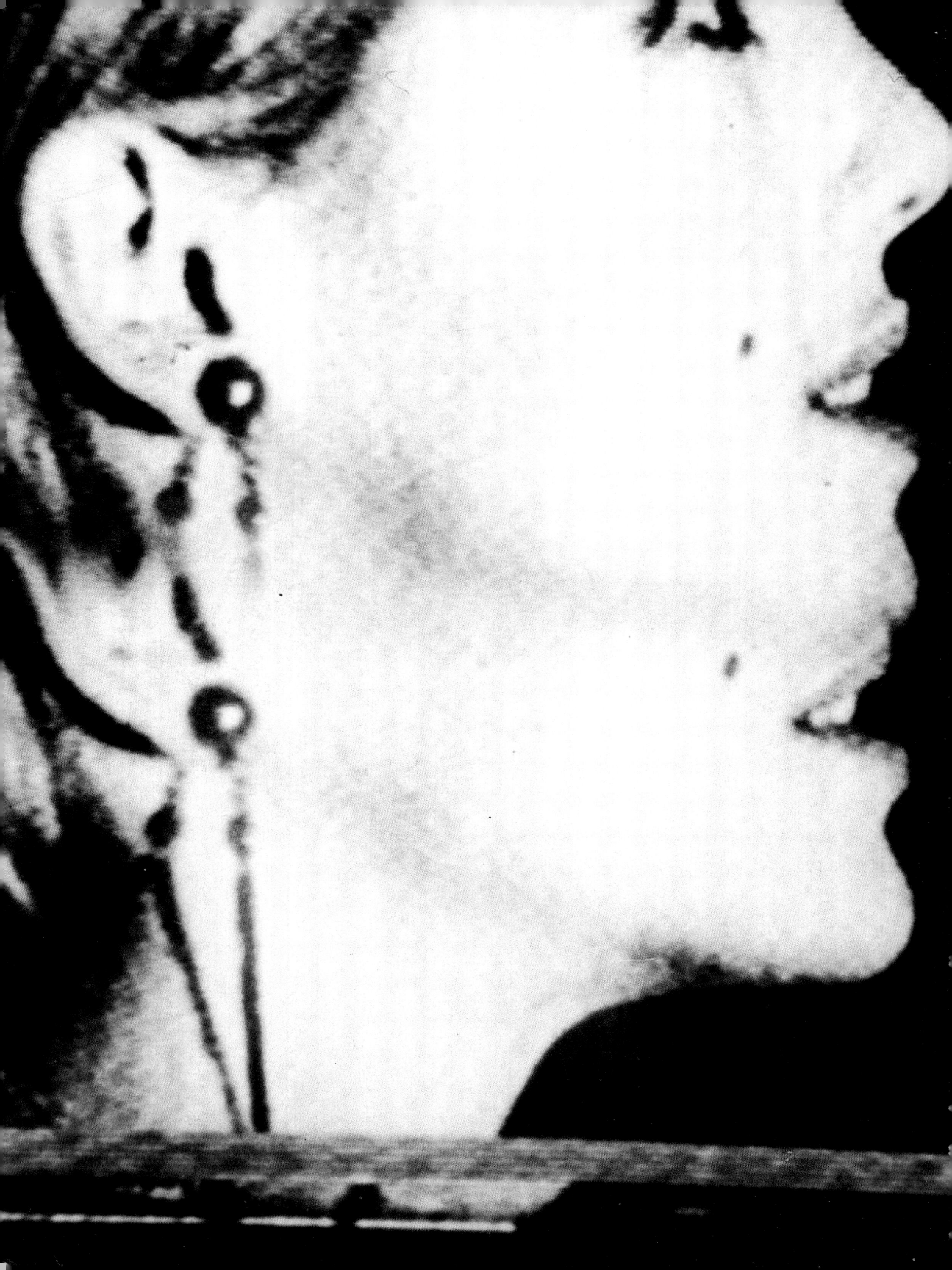